The Economics of International Ocean Transport
The Cuban Case before 1958

The Economics of International Ocean Transport

THE CUBAN CASE BEFORE 1958

By Claudio Escarpenter y Fargas

Translated from the Spanish
by Enrique Lerdau and Federico Lerdau

The University of Wisconsin Press
Madison and Milwaukee, 1965

*La Economía del Tráfico Marítimo
Internacional de Cuba* © 1958 by Claudio Escarpenter

Present edition in English © 1965 by
The Regents of the University of Wisconsin

PUBLISHED BY THE UNIVERSITY OF WISCONSIN PRESS
Madison and Milwaukee
P.O. Box 1379, Madison, Wisconsin 53701

Printed in the United States of America
by Kingsport Press, Inc., Kingsport, Tennessee

Library of Congress Catalog Card No. 65–16361

TO MY FATHER

AND THE MEMORY OF MY MOTHER

PREFACE

THE PUBLICATION IN 1958 of my book *La Economía del Tráfico Marítimo Internacional de Cuba* was the direct result of the circumstance that for two years I held a position in a Cuban shipping firm which enabled me to acquire first-hand knowledge of the industry. The economic interpretation of this information, in which I was aided by a number of specialists, was the basis of this study.

Professor Julián Alienes, then Director of the Department of Economic Research of the Banco Nacional de Cuba and Professor of Economic Policy at the University of Havana, who at present teaches at the University of Madrid, not only read in its entirety the draft of the Spanish edition, but also honored me by writing its Introduction; I have benefited greatly from his rigorously scholarly criticisms and suggestions, and I shall always be grateful for his kindness and encouragement. Dr. Luis José Abalo, a colleague at the University of Villanueva, who today is a teacher at the University of Caracas, also gave the final version a careful reading and pointed out several obscurities in the text. Similarly Dr. José Antonio Guerra, who is at present Deputy Director of the Department of Technical Cooperation of the Organization of the American States, and Dr. Felipe Pazos, now a member of the Panel of Experts of the Alliance for Progress, were good enough to read the final draft.

I am pleased to reiterate here the expression of gratitude contained in the Spanish edition to the shipping businessmen who cooperated so generously with my endeavors, to the distinguished economists mentioned above, to my statistical assistants, to the University of Santo Tomás de Villanueva (Havana), which decided to include my study among its publications and, finally, to the publishing house.

Circumstances were not propitious to making my book known, either at home or abroad. Because of my absence from Cuba and the suppression of the activities of the University of Villanueva, I do not know what became of most of the copies of the Spanish edition. Except for a few copies in my possession, I doubt that more than a hundred were ever distributed. The present edition can therefore be considered as the first one with any real possibility of reaching interested readers.

Messrs. Enrique and Federico Lerdau's translation is entirely faithful to the original text and in many instances improves on it in conciseness and precision. Anyone who has ever gone through a similar experience will recognize both the effort which the translators' careful labor represents, and the profound gratitude that it deserves.

After my book had gone to press in 1958, I had access to the report on *La Navegación Marítima Nacional de Cuba* (*Cuba's National Ocean Shipping*), prepared by the distinguished German economist Dr. Werner Nittscher, specialist in maritime matters. It was presented by the Hamburg shipyards, H. C. Stuelcken Sohn, to the Banco de Fomento Agrícola e Industrial de Cuba (Cuban Agricultural and Industrial Development Bank, or BANFAIC). Its analysis and both its explicit and implicit conclusions largely coincide with mine; often, in fact, the texts are so similar that the only explanation is that one and the same reality has twice been examined objectively and scientifically. The differences which exist are mainly questions of emphasis or of form.

I am not qualified to discuss the degree to which my study represents a contribution that goes beyond the Cuban situation of 1956. But although I would correct many shortcomings if I were to rewrite the book today, I do believe that the methods employed can be used in other underdeveloped countries. Therefore, although the book relates only to Cuba, perhaps it may nevertheless orient the analysis of the international maritime transport programs of such countries. Many of them seem inclined, for a variety of reasons, to look to the development of their merchant fleets as a major element in their general economic progress. This was noted also by P. Bellon,[1] who recommended a more cautious approach.

Another point of wider interest may be the facts presented in this book with regard to the organization and successful administration of shipping concerns by national—Cuban in this case—entrepreneurs. By exploiting some clear and natural advantages which they possessed over foreign firms, and by using the time-charter system to best advantage, these entrepreneurs were able to establish themselves and to hold their own against foreign competitors. Professor Alienes singled out this point in his Introduction to the Spanish edition and made the perspicacious comment that the book suggested the need to "discover a theory of maritime evolution of countries that start out from a position of complete dependence on foreign shipping enterprises and eventually reach the stage of maturity in which their merchant marine is owned, with but a few natural and justifiable exceptions, by nationals who operate the ships as well." Although I would be far from asserting that this evolution is the necessary course of events everywhere, I agree that its possibility is worth exploring and that, moreover, it may suggest a rational trial-and-error approach for countries that want to develop their embryonic merchant fleets, but find themselves limited by scarce resources.

In the English edition Professor Alienes' Introduction has been omitted because it was primarily addressed to the Cuban reader. Besides discussing the approach, scope, and limitations of the book, he predicted that my study would be controversial

1. See his "Marine Marchande et Pays en Voie de Developpement," *Revue Economique*, No. 4 (July, 1961).

in more than one respect. Experience has since proved him right; I have found that arguments like the ones here presented are not always received as calmly as one might wish. This edition may bear him out once more. I can do no more than repeat that in writing my book I had no other ambition than to follow the precept of *non fumum ex fulgore, sed ex fumo, lucem dare*. If the good faith be admitted with which I have tried to clarify matters that are often obscure, I will be highly gratified.

C. E.

Madrid
March, 1964

TRANSLATOR'S NOTE

I<small>N</small> 1961 I <small>HAD THE PLEASURE</small> of reviewing the Spanish edition of Dr. Escarpenter's book.[1] It was without much optimism that I concluded my review with a plea: "Finally, a word to the wealthy and wise. If this book were ever translated, it would inevitably suffer, for it is written with a truly Castillian grace and elegance of expression. Nevertheless, it would be a sign of shocking provincialism or lack of enterprise, if this study were not made accessible to students and civil servants of non-Spanish speaking nations. Foundations and publishers, please step forward!" I shot an arrow in the air . . . and, against all reasonable expectations, hit a target. Thanks to the initiative and imagination of the University of Wisconsin Press and of the Latin American Translation Program of the Association of American University Presses, my hope has become a reality and English readers will be able to avail themselves of a valuable case study, even though, as I foresaw, the author's elegance of style proved to be a challenge that the translators could not meet adequately.

Since my first wish has met with such unexpected fulfillment, I will now venture to express three more. One is that the book be read as a methodological model rather than because it deals with a country that happens to have appeared rather frequently in the daily headlines. It is as an essay in applied economics that it should be most valuable, not merely as background material on Cuba.

1. See *Kyklos* (1961), fasc. 4.

My second hope is that the conclusions of Dr. Escarpenter's inquiry not be transferred uncritically to other countries. It may well be that the same analysis in other cases will yield quite different results. What the book should do—and this was my reason for first suggesting a translation and then agreeing to collaborate in it—is to stimulate similar studies for other underdeveloped countries, and to set a standard for them. This standard cannot be better described than by using the words of a former President of the American Economic Association: ". . . calling shots as they really appear to be (on reflection and after weighing all evidences), even when this means losing popularity with the great audience of men and running against the 'spirit of the times'." [2]

The sense of guilt shared by my co-translator and myself for having converted the author's noble linguistic steed into a mere workhorse is tempered by my third hope: that even so, some readers may find the beast useful to plow unbroken earth. If so, our pains will have been repaid.

E. L.

Washington, D.C.
April, 1964

2. Paul A. Samuelson, "Economists and the History of Ideas," Presidential address delivered at the Seventy-Fourth Annual Meeting of the AEA. See *American Economic Review* LII (1) (March, 1962), 18.

CONTENTS

TABLES

CHARTS

The Economics of International Ocean Transport
The Cuban Case before 1958

1

THE BASIC STATISTICS

THE NATURE OF THIS STUDY is decidedly statistical. For this there are two reasons: on the one hand, we have to work with existing statistical data and, on the other, we have to come up with some new data ourselves. As far as the former are concerned, we must select the essential statistics that will help us to grasp the quantitative nature of the particular economic universe in which we are interested. We must dispel the errors that tend to prevail because the figures generally used in this connection are not the most relevant ones, are interpreted superficially or incorrectly, and are not correlated with other known information. But we will not merely gather data, published and unpublished, from primary sources; rather it will be our task—within the overall purpose of this inquiry—to construct new statistical tables with particular relevance for Cuba's international balance of payments on ocean transport account. There are therefore two separate statistical tasks: the first is elementary but unavoidable, while the second, more significant one, is to make an original contribution.

In the present chapter we shall restrict ourselves to the presentation, in a logical sequence, of primary data on the tonnages involved in Cuba's exports and imports by sea. Thus, for the time being, we will merely look at physical quantities, leaving the analysis of their money values—costs as well as freight rates—for later, when the role of Cuba's international maritime market is discussed. Knowing the volume and characteristics of the tonnage on the one hand, and the amounts of freight receipts and expenditures on the various cost-components on the other, and combining this information with some other variables, we will then be in a position to estimate approximately our chief statistical unknown: the balance of payments on ocean transport account. In the light of this, it need hardly be pointed out that beside the items mentioned we will have to collect some other figures as we go along, whenever they help to prove, justify, or confirm our theoretical or empirical reasoning about the economics of maritime transport, be it Cuba's or of the world economy.[1]

Regarding the data on tonnage, we will first present total exports and imports and then break them down into dry and liquid cargo according to the geographic distribution of incoming and outgoing traffic, as well as according to the commodity composition of the cargo. Furthermore, origins and ports of destination will be set down so that, eventually, the relative importance of particular routes can be deduced both according to geographic regions and according to the merchandise shipped. Thus it will gradually be possible to obtain an understanding of the flows of ocean trade between Cuba and the rest of the world. The sources for these data are official as well as private; the *Dirección de Estadística* of the Ministry of Finance for the former, and publications like *El Avisador* [2] for the latter. Sometimes the Ministry data are used exclusively and sometimes together with the figures from private sources. In the case of the analysis of tonnage by ports of origin and destination, since the Ministry does not supply the necessary information, data from *El Avisador* have been used.

---

1. Although the author collected a wealth of information on the tonnage, composition, and ports of origin and destination of the cargo shipped between Cuba and a large number of countries in 1956, it did not seem necessary to reproduce these data in their entirety in this book.

2. *El Avisador*, an export, import, and coastal trade bulletin, published daily in Havana, reproduces the manifestoes of all ships entering and leaving the port of Havana and some other Cuban ports. Several similar publications exist.

These, although not completely free from omissions and duplications, are the best available.

Limitations of time and resources have prevented us from constructing series with as wide a coverage as we would have wished. Thus the most complete set of data applies only to 1956. Therefore the main burden of the analysis in depth will fall on that year, although some tables for other years—less satisfactory in their design—will be used to help clarify particular points.

Tonnage Totals and Tonnages by Cargo

The first magnitudes to consider are total export and import tonnages. Total exports in 1956 reached 7,610,943 metric tons, amply surpassing total imports, which in that year, according to official sources, were 4,637,279 metric tons and, according to private sources, were slightly more, namely 4,670,950. Either figure may be accurate: what is certain is that exports exceeded imports by almost three million tons. This comparison by itself reveals something of interest about the imbalance between exported and imported cargo, but the figures require a more thorough analysis; only by establishing some important distinctions will we really understand the problem. One important distinction can be taken up immediately, namely that between dry cargo transported by ocean freighters or ferries and liquid cargo carried by tankers.

Total dry cargo exports in 1956 were 6,234,821 metric tons, a figure obtained by subtracting 1,376,122 metric tons from the total of 7,610,943. The subtracted amount represents exports of blackstrap molasses (593,753 tons), inverted molasses (737,856 tons), and inverted syrups (44,514 tons). Dry cargo imports were 2,525,502 tons, while the rest consisted of 2,145,-456 tons of petroleum and its products, including gasoline.

Thus the imbalance between import and export tonnages, which was noted above, becomes even larger when dry cargo alone is considered, since dry cargo exports in 1956 amounted to over six million tons, while imports were little more than 2,500,000 metric tons. While total export cargo exceeded total imports by 162 per cent, dry cargo exports were 246 per cent more than dry cargo imports.

These ratios are of great importance from several points of view, and must be taken into account in any serious analysis of Cuba's international ocean transport economy and also in making a correct appraisal of some domestic economic processes. For instance, it is interesting to see how the development and transformation of the economy over the years has affected the types of fuels used and, thereby, the types of ships needed for their importation. In 1911 Cuba imported some 1,020,000 metric tons of coal (mainly bituminous and coke) and in 1917 almost 1,500,000 tons; in 1956 she imported only about 50,000 metric tons, four-fifths of this total being coke and the remainder bituminous. In the meantime, the import of petroleum and its products went up from some 50,000 tons to approximately 2.2 million tons.[3] Consider what this implies with respect to the use of specialized ships such as tankers, as opposed to vessels with holds of all kinds, or in relation to the shifts in trade routes, in equipment and personnel used for cargo handling, and in the use of terminals.[4]

Geographic Distribution of Cuba's International Ocean Traffic

Having noted the overall totals of export and import tonnage, we turn to the geographic distribution of Cuba's international trade. For this, the most important distinction is between trade with the United States and trade with the rest of the world, because of the special economic nexus between Cuba and the United States, as well as their geographic proximity.

3. Information from the Ministry of Finance.
4. There are still people who remember the sight of Chinese coolies forming human chains to unload coal; the decay of the piers that used to receive coal shipments is visible to everyone.

In 1956 export tonnages amounted to 4,688,497 metric tons. In other words, 61.6 per cent of Cuba's total export volume went to the United States. In return Cuba in 1956 imported from the United States 2,422,930 tons, or 51.8 per cent of its total imports for the year. Again we must distinguish between dry and wet cargo. The total of Cuban dry cargo shipped to the United States in 1956 was 3,412,197 metric tons, while tankers carried over 1,276,300 tons (blackstrap and inverted molasses and inverted syrups). Imports of dry cargo from the United States in 1956 were on the order of 1,801,182 metric tons, that is to say, 74.34 per cent of total imports from the United States, while liquid cargo was 621,748 metric tons or 25.66 per cent of total imports originating in the United States.

Taking all other countries together, it can be noted that in 1956 they received from Cuba 2,822,624 tons of dry cargo and only 99,822 metric tons of liquid freight (molasses and syrups). On the other hand, Cuba's dry cargo imports from the rest of the world were only 724,230 tons (or 32.22 per cent), against wet cargo imports of 1,523,709 (or 67.78 per cent).

When we examine these figures certain facts stand out: (*a*) The United States is important to Cuba both as a buyer and a seller. (*b*) Although Cuba's dry cargo exports to the United States substantially exceed the tonnage of imports from this source, the disequilibrium is much larger in Cuba's trade with the rest of the world. (*c*) The tonnage of wet cargo imports exceeds that of wet cargo exports which are concentrated in the United States market (92.7 per cent of the total); three-fourths of wet cargo imports come from sources other than the United States (mainly from the Netherlands Antilles, and Venezuela).

These classifications and considerations underline the most important aspects of the overall picture. The distinction between dry and wet cargo highlights the most interesting point for our analysis: international sea transport of dry cargo. The transportation of wet cargo is a very specialized service and, in view of its low freight rates, is of limited importance; on the import side it is restricted to petroleum and its products, including gasoline. While the tonnage involved was shown to be about 45.9 per cent of total imports, the freight of $2.00 to $3.00 [5] per ton means that freight payments for liquid cargo may be no more than 6 to 8 per cent of total import freights. It follows that it is dry cargo freights that must mainly be of interest here, both because of their magnitude and because we need to know whether the savings on dry cargo freights produced by a national merchant marine are of an order to warrant advocating an effective policy in that direction.

Special Analysis of the Geographic Distribution of Dry Cargo

To put the subsequent analysis of dry cargo ocean transport into perspective, it will be useful to recapitulate the figures previously discussed. Table 1 and Chart I summarize these amounts, and Table 1 restates what was already noted: exports

TABLE 1

International Maritime Traffic of Cuba in 1956

(metric tons)

	United States	Other countries	Total
Exports:			
Liquid cargo	1,276,300	99,822	1,376,122
Dry cargo	3,412,197	2,822,624	6,234,821
Total	4,688,497	2,922,446	7,610,943
Imports:			
Liquid Cargo	621,748	1,523,709	2,145,456
Dry cargo	1,801,182	724,320	2,525,502
Total	2,422,930	2,248,029	4,670,959

Source: Ministry of Finance.

5. In the period from 1956 to 1958 the dollar and the peso were freely convertible on a one-to-one basis. They are therefore used interchangeably in this book.

CHART I
Cuba's International Maritime Traffic, 1956

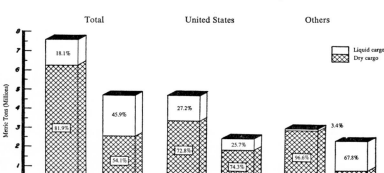

of dry cargo in 1956 amounted to a total of 6,243,821 metric tons, with tonnage destined for the United States exceeding that to other countries by 569,673 metric tons.

What types of merchandise did these exports consist of? Ministry of Finance data indicate that 81 per cent, or 2,755,485 tons of the total Cuban dry cargo destined for the United States consisted of sugar (raw, centrifugal, refined, and semirefined). For the rest of the world, sugar (crude and refined) was 91 per cent of the Cuban dry cargo export, or 2,586,738 metric tons. Thus, one cannot but notice the enormous share of sugar in Cuba's total export tonnage to the United States and its even larger share in trade with the rest of the world. Exports of minerals, fruits and vegetables, coffee, and tobacco account for most of the rest of the tonnage shipped to the United States, and these same products, plus an item labelled "unclassified" (69,712 tons), make up almost all other exports to the rest of the world.

It need hardly be stressed that the tremendous concentration of exports on one product, sugar, simplifies to a degree our task of understanding the general structure of Cuba's maritime traffic. Besides, the fact that usually over half of the sugar is exported to only one market, the United States, makes the analysis still easier, although the diversity of destination of the remaining sugar exports makes it extraordinarily difficult to be precise about the freights paid for the transportation to any particular country. But we do not intend to go that far, nor would there be any particular point to it in the context of this study; for the time being it will be quite sufficient to estimate an approximate average rate.

What is extremely important already—although more will be said about it later—is to stress that the large sugar shipments to the United States consitute a *potentially* attractive business for any shipping concern. Doubly so when it is remembered that this sugar goes to Eastern Seaboard and Gulf ports, from which most of Cuba's dry cargo imports from the United States are also shipped. Therefore, even though the total dry cargo exports and imports to and from the United States are unequal (3,392,197 metric tons exported against 1,801,182 imported), a well-organized shipping enterprise can nevertheless arrange for its vessels carrying Cuban sugar to the United States to return loaded, although not necessarily to their maximum capacity. Other combinations, to be mentioned later, are also possible. But before developing this further let us first examine the basic structure of dry cargo imports.

The degree of concentration of this traffic is even greater than that of exports, and again related to the United States. In 1956 some 1,801,182 tons of dry cargo were imported from the United States and only 724,320 from the rest of the world. It must be noted that the latter figure is distributed among more than a hundred countries, none of which provides 100,000 tons; only Canada, Germany, and Belgium exceeded 50,000 tons in 1956.

It is unnecessary therefore to go further into the high concentration of Cuban imports which in such an overwhelming proportion originate in the United States. But even there the geographic concentration is actually still more acute, since by far the largest part of United States merchandise sold to Cuba is shipped through Atlantic and Gulf ports. When in the last chapter of this book we refer to the possibilities and limitations of any deliberate policy designed to foster a national merchant fleet, it will become clear how much the consideration of the location of the main foreign ports circumscribes such a policy and puts a brake on the flights of our fancy.

The high concentration of points of origin similarly facilitates the study of the economic structure of Cuba's ocean import traffic. Here we no longer deal with a homogeneous product, like sugar, but with a broad range of goods extending from raw materials to the most elaborate equipment. Nevertheless, since there is a distinct grouping of types of merchandise by zones, ports of origin, and points of destination—and hence according to shipping routes—the short- and medium-term analysis of the matter is less complex than it might appear. For example, in the United States, shipments from Albany are entirely of bulk spring wheat; those from New York, as might be expected, consist mostly of manufactured products; and those originating in the Gulf of Mexico are mainly agricultural products. This does not mean that ports north of Cape Hatteras do not ship important agricultural items (potatoes, for instance) or unprocessed raw materials, nor that we do not receive from the South of the United States an increasing volume of industrial goods.[6] Other ports, Charleston, for example, are characterized by the high proportion which a few items—textiles, pulp, and paper in this case—represent in their total shipments

6. The economic development of the Southeast of the United States, spurred largely by World War II, is providing a growing volume of manufactured goods to be exported to Cuba; this trade is added to that in rice, which since 1937 has developed greatly. On the economic development of the Southeast of the United States, see Charles T. Taylor, "Income Growth in the Southern United States since 1929 as a Model of Economic Development," in *Proceedings, Fourth Meeting of Technicians of Central Banks of the American Continent, Board of Governors of the Federal Reserve System* (Washington, D.C., 1955), I, 369–94.

to Cuba. Others, such as those with ferry service, export goods for which the use of tanker wagons is particularly appropriate.

Finally, it must be observed that the number of Cuba's ports is large relative to the total volume moving through them. The tonnages corresponding to each port in 1956 are shown in Table 2. Even a cursory examination of the distribution of

TABLE 2
Traffic of Cuba's Main Ports in 1956
(metric tons)

Port	Imports	Exports
Antilla	118,382	792,407
Banes	8,568	74,518
Baracoa	152	71,421
Caibarién	8,804	391,498
Cárdenas	43,217	402,602
Cienfuegos	124,841	539,968
General Peraza	4,297	344,588
Gibara	12,176	71,921
Guantánamo	14,079	274,158
Havana	3,248,309	737,854
Júcaro	1,312	498,150
Manzanillo	9,158	197,219
Mariel	175,556	272,845
Matanzas	224,581	327,253
Nueva Gerona	633	—
Nuevitas	203,089	1,098,426
Puerto Padre	23,952	495,837
Santa Cruz del Sur	1,061	283,137
Santiago de Cuba	432,647	632,312
Trinidad	16,145	112,434

Source: Ministry of Finance.

exports and imports among the twenty ports clearly shows the imbalance of export and import tonnages; the ports with the largest exports are not those where imports are largest. In this regard the case of Havana is very instructive even without considering the traffic in liquid cargo.

The importance of this phenomenon is that it thus becomes practically impossible for ships operating on Cuba's international routes to do so at their lowest cost, since they will often have to carry ballast, for lack of export freight in some cases and lack of import cargo in others. For the development of an efficient international merchant marine—and, be it noted, only for this—the abundance of excellent ports on Cuba's coasts is not an advantage, as is commonly believed, but rather the opposite.[7] Let us take note then of how tenuously based are some propositions which have acquired the status of supposedly irrefutable arguments. Remember that during World War II the policy of concentration of shipments through a limited number of ports was adopted not only for strategic reasons (convoys travelling under military protection), but also because the most efficient utilization of the available vessels became more important than such costs as those of internal transport and distribution.

7. If the traffic to be developed were coastal, the opposite conclusion would apply.

2

CUBA'S INTERNATIONAL
OCEAN FREIGHT MARKET

IN THIS CHAPTER we shall try to outline the basic structure of Cuba's international maritime freight market. In other words, we will discuss the structural characteristics and the economic forces that determine the price (freight rates) of this service. This will also help us to understand some fundamental points about the real possibilities for a national merchant marine.

We may begin with a conclusion: Cuba possesses an excellent international ocean cargo service. This bold and general assertion will later be explained in detail by spelling out in what particular sense it may be accepted.

Being an island, Cuba needs a good maritime transport service. As air transport becomes increasingly economical it will undoubtedly grow in importance, but for the foreseeable future ocean transport will remain vital for the national economy.[1] Also, Cuba is a country with an open economy, that is to say, with a strongly export-oriented production on which the level of its national income largely depends. And the latter in turn determines the country's large imports. These two circumstances not only create the absolute necessity for an adequate international ocean service, but also account for its existence. This is true because the magnitude, whether measured

1. For a brief discussion of the development of international air freight service and its unpredictable future, see "Air Transport Looks Ahead," *Shipping Times and Air Transport,* No. 1 (May, 1955), pp. 46 ff. The main difficulty is return cargo.

in volume or in value, of the exports and imports requiring transportation is sufficient to offer an attractive payload—to use a trade term—to a very considerable number of interested vessels of many nationalities.

Besides—or, if one prefers, because of—Cuba's structural characteristic of being a very open economy, the island enjoys a particularly advantageous geo-economic location. Situated at the entrance of the Gulf of Mexico, east of the United States, and in a manner of speaking in the center of today's economic Mediterranean, the Atlantic Ocean, it makes payloads even more attractive by being on or near the world's great ocean trade routes. Consider the implications on traffic potential of the large and continuous trade between European or Asiatic ports and those on the Gulf of Mexico, or of the many routes linking the Eastern Seaboard of the United States with South American ports, or, for that matter, the implications of the island's location near the Panama Canal! [2]

On the other hand, to the extent that the economic development of many countries is accompanied by a growing foreign trade, it will imply an increase in the cargoes shipped over routes that pass near the island. This would presumably in-

2. The *Daily Freight Record* (New York), July 24, 1957, gave the following statistics on use of the Panama Canal. The freight tonnage moving through the Canal during fiscal year 1957 was about twice that of the annual average of the decade preceding World War II. It amounted to 50,000,000 tons against a previous record of 46,000,000. The number of vessels in excess of 300 tons and the total Canal revenues also reached new heights. Fiscal 1957 was the sixth consecutive year in which previous records were exceeded. During the depression, the war, and the postwar years until 1952, the 1929 level was not surpassed; but the 8579 ships— excluding those of the United States government, as well as coastal and pleasure craft—which used the Canal in 1957 represented an increase of 36 per cent over the 6289 vessels in 1929. Total transit fees collected in 1957 were $2,200,000 more than in 1956 and consisted of $39,653,712 from commercial users and $1,140,116 from payments for United States government shipments. Of the 50,624,373 tons of freight that were transported through the Canal in fiscal 1957, only 929,173 were government shipments.

crease the number of ships willing to touch our ports, provided of course that general and specific economic conditions
in Cuba are such as to ensure a remunerative level of freight
rates.[3]

If these factors—freight volume and favorable geo-economic
location—help Cuba enjoy a satisfactory international ocean
freight service, it would seem logical to conclude that this
service as well as the freight rates charged, must be competitive. Although it will be found later that this conclusion
is approximately correct, it would be premature to accept it
definitively without an examination of the actual market
structure and its determinants. For this it will first be necessary
to outline the main features of maritime economics, such as
the types of ships and services in use, the structures of the
main individual markets, and the character of their respective
freight rates. Having done this in the necessary detail, we will
then try to trace the morphology of the Cuban maritime market,
on the basis of the distinction between export and import trade.
This will show the significant differences between the two
freight rate markets, which in turn produce certain peculiarities
in the overall picture of Cuba's international maritime market.

The General Structure of Ocean Freight Markets

To sketch the basic traits and behavior of ocean transport
markets, let us begin by analyzing the meaning of the distinction between the two main types of transport by sea, that
supplied by "tramp" or "free navigation" vessels and that in
the hands of "regular service" or "line" ships. If the significance of this distinction is fully explored, the economic charac-

3. The existence of regular passenger routes permits the transportation
of cargo as a sideline over routes that by themselves would be only
moderately attractive. The service between Spain and Cuba is a case in
point.

teristics of the corresponding freight rates will also be evident and it will become possible to describe the structure of both markets.

Tramps are vessels used to transport complete cargoes of foodstuffs (cereals, sugar, chick-peas, rice, etc.) and of coal, wood, fertilizers, minerals, etc.[4] Transactions in such commodities are usually carried on between large-scale operators who buy and sell substantial amounts.

The international markets of such goods are usually subject to considerable instability. This affects both the volumes and the directions of trade and is caused, especially on the short run, by the erratic behavior of weather and harvests. At the same time, supplies are usually concentrated in the hands of large-scale sellers who may buy from smaller producers and sell to foreign processors or distributors who also tend to operate on a large scale.

Because they handle sizeable consignments of particular primary products, the large-scale operators have an interest in being able to charter ships on an irregular basis that is easily adjustable to fluctuations in demand and sales opportunities. This is one reason why ordinarily they do not use lines with fixed sailing schedules; they will utilize them in particular instances, but not on a stable or permanent basis. On the other hand, when necessary, these large-scale operators will tend to shop around among shipowners to obtain the broadest possible range of options regarding ports of loading and unloading within a coastal zone whose amplitude varies with market conditions. In other words, the relative bargaining power of the parties at any particular moment determines how much

4. In a broader sense one may here also include the transportation of liquid fuels—crude oil and gasoline—and even certain other goods. See Frank M. Fisser, *Trampschiffahrt Entwicklung, Bedeutung, Marktelemente —Trampshipping Development, Significance, Market Elements* (English-German edition; Bremen: Weltschiffahrts-Archiv, 1957), pp. 55 *et passim,* and A. C. Hardy, et al., *The Bulk Cargoes* (London: Coram Publishers Ltd., 1954).

flexibility will be conceded to the operators, although normal usage sets some limits on the range within which this bargaining operates. A big shipper may also try to reserve himself the right to declare [5] the port of unloading only after a more or less lengthy time during which he may await market developments after the merchandise has already been loaded. This will create for him a saving on storage account. Naturally, the length of the time period varies with the duration of the voyage from the producing country's port or ports to those of the country of destination. A case in point is the difference between sugar shipments to the United States from Cuba and from the Philippines. Probably the range of options and the delay in "declaring" are much greater in the case of the latter country.

This, in brief, is the primary reason for the transportation of internationally traded bulk food and raw materials by tramp vessels. Now let us examine the characteristics of regular lines with fixed sailing schedules.

These lines operate on routes over which a more heterogeneous freight is shipped, which is usually traded in many relatively small transactions by numerous buyers or sellers, although not necessarily by both. While this definition is not given in the standard works consulted, we venture to suggest that it is the one best suited to modern economic analysis. It tells us that regular liners normally do not transport complete loads or large volumes of homogeneous products, but rather tend to specialize in merchandise in which each good is only a small proportion of the total tonnage. Such goods usually have high unit values and high price and income elasticities of demand. They are traded under economic and institutional conditions different from those applying to primary products. The regularity and frequency of the service, as well as the right to its utilization, are important parts of their transportation.

5. To "declare" is to specify definitely the port in which unloading or loading is to occur, choosing one port from those listed in the options given by the charter contract.

Naturally, even though the above are the basic determinants, truly regular services could not exist without the concurrence of some technical factors affecting the ships and some economic conditions related to the enterprises. The former concern the sources of energy by which ships are moved. Clearly, before the advent of steam power, sailing vessels could not guarantee schedules with the reliability of regular lines; but once engines replaced sails, fixed departure times and lengths of voyages could be established. And as long as there are users who are interested in having regular service, the shipping concerns will be interested in providing it if it yields them enough income to stay in business. By virtue of this fact, on routes on which more than one regular line operates, they have with increasing frequency entered into agreements, usually known as "conferences."

A shipping conference is an association of regular-line operators. Its purpose is (1) to regulate competition among members and (2) to strengthen them through concerted action in their struggle against non-members.[6] Actually, success in its second objective will facilitate achievement of the first since it proves the efficacy of joint action against independent operators. The conference system among lines has grown impressively since its beginning in 1875 on the Great Britain–Calcutta route, so much so that on some routes no independent operator remains.

Since in this study the emphasis is on an analysis of the market from the vantage point of economic theory, the administrative and legal practices of conferences need not be described. More deserving of study here are the economic forces making for the creation and more or less stable maintenance of conferences.

Theoretically, shipping conferences are just another example of the imperfect competition that prevails in the contemporary economy. They are formed by a small number of firms, i.e.,

6. William L. Grossman, *Ocean Freight Rates* (Cambridge, Md.: Cornell Maritime Press, 1956), p. 62.

by duopolies or oligopolies. In the case of regular routes, the two or more firms providing a transport service cannot by definition offer a significantly differentiated product or service, even though managements may, either inside or outside conferences, try to compete by attending to the special needs of users. This is particularly true for cargo transport; passenger service presumably can be somewhat more differentiated. Although personal and friendly relations may exist between shippers and users and such differentiating features as the care with which cargoes are handled, the quality of pier and warehouses, the attention which claims for damage may receive, etc., it is unlikely that such differences could create enough customer loyalty to permit lasting price—i.e., freight rate—gaps.

Thus, no more than faint shades of difference can exist in the product (service) offered. Therefore price (freight rate) differences on a given route would act decisively to determine the customer's choice of line.[7] Under open competition, price wars would harm both users and line operators. Such rate wars give the users short-term gains, but if they end with the disappearance of one or several of the competing lines, the victor or victors will be left with greater monopolistic rate-fixing power. And this power will be used to recoup the losses suffered in the price war by raising freight rates to whatever level the market will bear. Moreover, violent rate fluctuations not only upset the stability of the shipping business, but also in varying degrees that of the users. Both, therefore, tend to accept agreements for rate maintenance as being, at worst, the lesser evil.

Shipping Conferences as Oligopolistic Agreements

After the preceding rough outline of the system of conferences, a section of this chapter will be devoted to an attempt

7. This is true particularly if the lines have similar or identical arrival and departure dates.

to match the actual workings of this system with the economic theory dealing with the thorny problem of oligopolistic equilibrium. For this we choose Professor William Fellner's recent formulation.[8] Although somewhat of a digression, such a comparison is distinctly useful, since it has the advantage of proving a very satisfactory correlation between theory and practice, between the world of business and the world of books. And this will help the student of either to find enlightenment in the other.

A seller—in this case a line operator—who is a member of the small group labelled "oligopoly" by modern economic theory, does not work along a Marshallian supply curve derived from the technical conditions of production. Rather, he tries to select a particular price to be charged and a particular quantity to be sold, and to maximize his income in the process. But the amount he can sell at a particular price will depend partly on the prices charged by his competitors and this in turn will be influenced by his own price; similarly the amount he can sell at any price will depend on the amount marketed by his competitors, i.e., by the amount that they can produce and sell at that price. Consequently the oligopolist neither operates on a single supply curve, nor is he faced by a demand curve that can be defined exclusively as a function of con-

8. William Fellner, *Competition Among the Few, Oligopoly and similar Market Structures* (New York: Alfred A. Knopf, 1949). A Spanish version has been published by the Fondo de Cultura Económica, Mexico, 1953. There is so much in this book that is applicable to the analysis of oligopolistic shipping markets, that it might have been written with them in mind. This was also observed by Daniel Marx, Jr., who, in his *International Shipping Cartels* (Princeton: Princeton University Press, 1953), p. 251, writes: "Professor Fellner's observations on spontaneous coordination, the maximization of joint profits, and the limitations thereto contain penetrating insights which appear to the author to provide the beginning of a systematic explanation of the formation of shipping conferences and the activities of their rate committees." He adds further that "a complete theory of shipping conferences may also be derived some day from John Von Neumann's and Oskar Morgenstern's *Theory of Games and Economic Behavior* (Princeton University Press, 1947)."

sumers' preferences, i.e., in our case those of the users of shipping on the routes in question.

It would appear then that no single equilibrium point can be determined for such a firm, if by that term we mean one derived directly from the demand and supply functions or, more fundamentally, from utility functions and technical cost conditions. A minimum boundary does of course exist for this area of indeterminacy. It is the long-term zero profits level. But above it lies a range of varying amplitude whose upper limit is provided by the market demand function.

It should be stressed that the core of the difficulty is that traditional economic analysis only provides us with adequate tools if we can make the assumption that "what I will want to do" will be determined by "what I assume the other parties' reaction will be," but not the reverse. The tools become inadequate if what I will want to do depends on my assumption about my opponents' reactions and at the same time the other parties want to let their decisions depend on what they guess my reaction will be. Fellner [9] points out that this situation in which everybody's behavior depends on everybody's assumptions about everybody else's reactions typically leads to "bargaining." It implies the existence of a "conjectural interdependence" in which each firm tries to sound out the reaction of the others, either by trial and error or by direct contacts and negotiations.

The bargaining power of the parties depends on factors which Fellner groups under the following headings:

a) Long-run consequences of violating accepted value judgments (that is, of faring too well);

b) The immediate political consequences of a stalemate in the relations between the parties concerned;

c) The ability of the parties to take and to inflict losses during stalemates;

9. *Competition Among the Few,* p. 15 *et passim.*

d) Toughness in the sense of unwillingness to yield in a range in which the other party is expected to yield if one fails to do so.[10]

The first of these categories involves quasi-ethical social value judgments. To prosper at the expense of the rest may be considered improper beyond certain limits. The second factor involves consideration of the public interest, to which "cutthroat competition" may be considered detrimental. Sometimes the battle would be much more violent if there were no fear of intervention by the public authorities when the public welfare is involved. The third factor is self-explanatory and is related to the preceding ones. Businesses differ not only in their capacity to support losses but also in their ability to inflict them, depending on the size of their assets, their liquidity, the quality of their organization and management, etc.

Commenting on the first three factors Fellner observes that

the first (*a*) may in many instances prevent a party from realizing immediate "advantages" which otherwise would be available in the short run. The second and third —(*b*) and (*c*)—relate to the consequences of *temporary* stalemates, and they provide criteria by which it is possible to judge the advisability or inadvisability of avoiding *temporary* stalemates at certain costs. If these three factors are correctly appraised, and are known to be correctly appraised by all parties, their effect is to reduce the range of indeterminateness lying between the limits determined by the usual kind of cost (or zero-profit) considerations. With mutually correct appraisal of the first three factors and of the zero-profit limits, the outcome in the remaining range depends exclusively on each party's appraisal of the other party's psychological properties as compared with its own.[11]

10. *Ibid.*, pp. 24–28.
11. *Ibid.*, p. 28.

The consequences of factor *d,* the reluctance to yield, will differ according to how correctly the first three factors and the zero-profit level are appraised. If the mutual evaluations are incorrect, very aggressive competition may develop in which each firm may try to break its rivals even at the cost of high short-run sacrifices. This may in turn lead to a reappraisal by each party of the other's qualities, new concessions may be made, and a tacit or explicit agreement may be reached.

Now if factors *a, b,* and *c* and the zero-profit level are correctly appraised by the parties from the beginning, equilibrium will be reached much more easily. Certainly when the competing firms are well acquainted with each other and, more importantly, when from this knowledge of each other and of the prevailing "extra-market" [12] operations, stable rules of conduct have already emerged, the danger of errors of appraisal that will provoke disagreements diminishes. In the case of active and dynamic enterprises, on the other hand, the possibility of such mistaken judgments increases and disequilibrium becomes more likely.

In any event, in oligopolistic markets like those of routes serviced by regular shipping lines, there is a clear tendency for agreements to emerge. That is to say, conferences are likely to be formed by the firms strong enough to survive the pre-conference environment and to enforce the agreement once it has been entered into.

It was pointed out above that because substantial product (service) differentiation is not possible, the agreement affects primarily the variable with the greatest impact on competition, namely, the price. Typically, therefore, the conference takes the form of two or more line operators joining to fix a common freight rate to be charged. But although service differentiations are less important than price differences, a wide range of

12. We use the expression "extra-market" in the same sense as the Australian economist E. Ronald Walker does in *From Economic Theory to Policy* (Chicago: The University of Chicago Press, 1943; 2nd impression, 1947), p. 100 *et passim.*

possibilities does exist in this area. Thus the good reputation that one of the oligopolists may have earned and may manage to keep up, and, more particularly, the efforts exerted to solicit cargoes permit rather intensive competitive activities. A close examination of these factors shows the high degree of dynamism that the management of shipping enterprises need merely to maintain their existing market shares. Sometimes this dynamism causes the threat or actual occurrence of a breach, so that an open struggle ensues. Such struggles may end with the disappearance of one of the combatants, with the re-establishment of the *status quo ante* or a modification of the agreement, or with another agreement in which the total freight, or the income that it produces, is parceled out among the participants. The last solution mentioned results then in a dual agreement, one part concerning rates and the other concerning revenues. The conference then becomes a pool, and service differentiation no longer has much purpose. The services rendered by the participants are then so coordinated as to offer transportation with the necessary regularity but without excess capacity. The participants thus are likely to reduce their costs somewhat.

The conference as well as the pool will try—though not necessarily succeed [13]—to maximize group profits. Their distribution will then be made according to each member's bargaining power, i.e., according to the factors *a, b, c,* and *d* discussed above. "This proposition," says Fellner, and our experience bears him out,

> follows directly from the assumption (and from the observed fact) that bargaining "normally" leads to an agreement. When it does the parties will surely not be indifferent to the size of the pie they are now dividing. Jointly they have the size of the pie under control. *They are, of course, subject to limitations imposed by cost functions and by*

13. In the case of pools, the tighter links among group members permit a closer approximation to joint profit maximization than simple conferences do.

buyers preferences, but these need not be stressed because they are taken for granted when we speak of the maximization of the joint profits. The maximization of the joint profit means that the *bargaining ranges are determined by the traditional functions of value theory* in such a way that for each firm the upper limit is set by the possibility of obtaining for itself the entire (maximized) joint profit, while the lower limit is at the zero profit level.[14]

We have italicized some phrases in the preceding quotation to underscore what indeed must be perfectly obvious to anyone even slightly acquainted with business or economics. This is, that the price or rate charged by oligopolists will always be directly related to the cost of producing the good or service and the demand for it.

It is true that an area of indeterminacy exists, within which the parties will exert their bargaining power and will try to obtain maximum advantages. But in oligopoly group situations this area will always be bounded by the following two criteria, which are also mentioned by Fellner. One is that businessmen will usually forego profit maximization "today" if it imperils tomorrow's profits enough to make the total profits over both periods smaller than they would have been without short run maximization. We will see below that for firms of modest size, such as Cuban ship operators, the rental of vessels instead of the use of their own ships limits their risks for the future to a degree that influences their profits for "today." The second one is that maximum profits are not a definitely ascertainable amount, nor can the strategy needed to obtain them be specified with any certainty according to known rules. Instead, one has a notion of *expected* or probable profits, arrived at on the basis of past experience and continuously subject to new shadings. Only hypothetically does the accumulation of such experience yield a uniform set of decision rules. In practice these rules are good, but not perfect, guides in

14. *Ibid.,* p. 33. Italics added.

the search for maximum profits. The achievement of maximum profits within the bargaining range is thus likely to be fortuitous and transitory at best, even though as a goal it will always be important.

Theory and practice reach the same conclusion on this point and it is a good sign for the former that a comparison of them should produce this impression so overwhelmingly. But it also speaks well for the firms and their directors that in the dynamic world of business they appear to act "as if" they were guided by theoretical formulae. And yet, although quite a few economists may doubt or deny this, we should not really be surprised, for it was one of the pillars of our profession, Alfred Marshall, who in his *Principles of Economics* indicated that "the side of life with which economics is specially concerned is that in which man's conduct is most deliberate, and in which he most often reckons up the advantages and disadvantages of any particular action before he enters on it." [15] Moreover, continues the Cambridge sage, "it is that side of life in which, when he does follow habit and custom, and proceeds for the moment without calculation, the habits and customs themselves are most nearly sure to have arisen from a close and careful watching the advantages and disadvantages of different courses of conduct."

Freight Rates

We have gradually penetrated into the structure of the market for maritime freight transportation. Above all, we have established the distinction between tramp and line services on the basis of differences in types of merchandise carried and user's needs. These two conditions, kind of freight and shipper's requirements, make it possible that in some cases transport services are provided irregularly and in others by regular

15. Alfred Marshall, *Principles of Economics* (8th ed.; New York: Macmillan Co., 1949), pp. 20–21.

lines. In the latter case, one or more concerns may service a particular route. The number is, of course, limited by the cargo potential of the route and is rarely much above two. Thus, the more important regular line routes tend to be serviced by oligopolistic groups that usually are driven by almost unavoidable economic pressures to enter into agreements. These in turn may be uniform freight rate "conferences" or, less frequently, "pools" in which the route's total tonnages or revenues are shared out by some formula among the participants.

We have tried to elucidate the theoretical bases for the existence and general form and conditions of these agreements, thus providing, we hope, a good example of what explanatory power modern economic theory can bring to bear on such problems. Finally, we have tried to sketch briefly the underlying market structure for maritime freights, which in turn makes it possible to explain the prevailing market prices (rates). Actually we do not deal with a single market but with several or many, and although this has already been stated, we will stress it even further below. Nevertheless, it should also be remembered that there are so many links and connections between these markets, that a clear picture becomes difficult to draw. When, as is frequently the case, routes of competitors coincide only in particular segments and differ in others, one may even argue that no clearly definable common spatial market exists, and in such cases equilibrium analysis in terms of oligopolistic competition breaks down.

FREIGHT RATES IN TRAMP MARKETS

Freight rates, like any other prices, are a function of demand and supply conditions in particular markets. The latter may be more or less competitive and we have already seen that in ocean freight transportation the degree of competition varies widely. It ranges from almost perfect competition in the tramp traffic to imperfect competition and quasi-monopoly in routes serviced by regular lines.

Again, size and number must be taken into account. The tramp business is generally in the hands of concerns with small numbers of ships.[16] In view of the extensiveness of this service internationally, it therefore follows that the number of firms rendering it must be very large, and each of them relatively small in size. Furthermore, aside from the type of cargoes they transport, another characteristic of tramp ships is their great locational mobility, because they must be responsive to shifts in the demand for the commodities which they carry. Consequently, subject to the qualifications to be made below, the large number of tramp operators are not usually faced with a few "oligopsonistic"[17] buyers, since the general "non-specialization" of these vessels allows their owners or operators to choose among the many shippers of the various types of merchandise requiring this kind of transportation. In other words, because the tramp operator can in most cases transport cereals as well as coal, fertilizer, sugar, or many other such products, he also faces a competitive market on the demand side.

However, the degree of market competition declines as specialization rises, be it on the supply or on the demand side. Concerning the former we have already pointed out that ships are not totally homogeneous, if only because they differ according to tonnage, speed, cargo handling equipment, etc.[18] This

16. See Emery Troxel, *Economics of Transport*, (New York: Rinehart, 1955), p. 420.

17. This label corresponds to widening the concept of the single buyer, or "monopsonist," to refer to a number in excess of, but not much in excess of, two. See Joan Robinson, *The Economics of Imperfect Competition* (London: Macmillan Co., 1950), p. 215.

18. An owner may also prefer to have his vessel operate in a particular region. This localizes and reduces his market, at least over the short and medium term. Nevertheless, there may be reasons for such a preference, such as distance from the home port or from the owner's center of operations, general or specific guarantees of charterers in each zone, or a vessel so new that repairs and adjustments still fall under builder's warranties, in which case proximity to the construction docks may be advantageous. In addition, particular zones or ports may attract crews more easily, either because of the length of the voyage or because of other advantages.

differentiation on the supply side affects demand because different routes have varying requirements for vessels of particular
speed, carrying capacity, or cargo-handling equipment, at least
within certain limits. To this may be added that, on the demand
side, once an operator has chosen to handle a particular type
of cargo—albeit the most advantageous one to him—frequently
the degree of competition facing him is reduced since the
number of shippers of the commodity in question may be
small. Then the freight rate charged will, within certain limits,
depend on the bargaining power of the parties. In reality the
problem is quite complex: the market may be competitive, but
not perfectly so. Partial equilibrium analysis in that case does
not really explain market behavior conclusively. We may therefore have here an example of the limitations of applying this
theoretical tool to situations of imperfect competition.

In any event, competition in the tramp market, while not
perfect, is vigorous, as witnessed by the transfer of vessels from
one route to another and from one kind of cargo to another
when relative demand or freight rates change.[19] There are
therefore at all times "marginal" vessels, and these will determine the prevailing rate levels both for voyage charters and
for time charters.

The two types of ship rentals create another market imperfection, although, since close connections exist between them,
only on the short run. W. Arthur Lewis [20] explains this interrelation: "Time charter rates are linked with voyage charter
rates both on the supply side and on the demand side. On the
supply side the shipowner has the alternative of seeking a
time or a voyage charter. On the demand side some merchants

---

19. Although differences in carrying capacity also limit competition between tramp ships, a decline in the demand for large boats tends to be
transmitted also to the smaller ones. When the former have no customers
for full cargoes, they will begin to accept incomplete ones, so that, step
by step, the smaller vessels are also affected.

20. "The Interrelation of Shipping Freights" in his *Economics of Overhead Costs* (New York: Rinehart, 1949), p. 91.

are indifferent as between time and voyage charters, and even if this were not so, speculators would take ships on time charter and re-let them on voyage charter if the former rate were out of step. The two rates must therefore move together." We would add that, were it not for the possibility of speculation by the shipper or the owner, or even by third parties, there would be no difference between the price of a charter for one voyage and that for several (for a specified time). It seems logical that in the absence of speculation no separate time and voyage charter markets could exist, but only the latter. But since speculation—forecasting market developments and acting accordingly—always does exist, there will always be price differences between the two markets. Things could be different if expectations ceased to exist, or if they were identical on the demand and on the supply side.

Nevertheless it should be made clear that such speculation is not always voluntary; in certain circumstances it is even "forced" upon the ship operator. Typically this occurs when he operates chartered vessels on routes which have regular service in one direction but not in the other. Then the requirements of the regular service will force him to charter boats for longer than the duration of one voyage, that is to say, to enter the time charter market.

Another set of considerations might be cited to underline the competitive nature of the tramp market, as well as the limitations of that competition. These deal with inter-temporal adjustments of supply and of demand, with the estimates of different managers, and with the differences in costs—with special reference to labor costs and fiscal contributions and subsidies—created by differences in the nationalities of vessels. But our purpose here is simply to make clear what the degree of competition in this market really is. Competition is active and vigorous, but not perfect; it is well known that no market in modern economies reaches that ideal and unrealistic state.

One further important feature of this market must be considered, that is, its instability. It is subject to seasonal, cyclical, and random fluctuations around an apparent long-term trend toward a reduction of the share of tramps in the overall tonnage transported by international maritime freight services. There are several causes of this tendency, but prominent among them is the more or less artificial growth of national merchant fleets.

The fluctuations of tramp freight rates of course follow closely the vagaries of demand for the transported commodities. Since they usually move together, the instability of c.i.f. (cost, insurance, and freight) prices of such commodities becomes accentuated. However, for a number of reasons—especially because the supply elasticity of ships tends to be less than that of the transported goods—the two series are not perfectly synchronized.[21]

FREIGHT RATES IN THE LINER MARKET

The regular liner market has already been described as monopolistic. But the extent to which competition is restricted varies, so that some freight rates will be further removed than others from a long-run equilibrium level in which costs, including normal competitive profits, are barely covered.

A comparison with the railroads may illustrate that even when a maritime route is serviced by only one line, the freight rate can hardly reach the monopolistic level that might be charged by a railroad.

21. Fluctuations of free shipping charter quotations have become more violent in the postwar period. Two main reasons account for this: (a) intervention in the commodity markets by governments offering, withholding, or buying large volumes of such products has created new and practically unforeseeable oscillations in the demand for tramp shipping; and (b) the growing tendency of shippers to own their own fleets or to hold substantial long-term time charters has made the market for shorter charters more supplemental and marginal and subject to the most violent ups and downs of rates. Among tankers, on the other hand, the opposite tendency seems to be at work, with the share of independent operators rising.

Once the latter is built, and the initial advantages which the expectation of its appearance provide have been exploited, these advantages will remain or even grow. If the route chosen is optimal, all other roads that might be constructed subsequently are, necessarily, inferior. By way of contrast, the ocean does not provide an exclusive route to anyone, so that even when one enterprise has chosen an optimum location, the possibility of *entry* by other firms always remains. Therefore the line that operates alone on a given route cannot, for any length of time, afford to charge rates high enough to make entry attractive to competitors. But for this threat, the freight rate charged would lie on the user's market-demand curve; as it is, the rate that assures the monopolist maximum long-term profits will be considerably below this curve. Sometimes—in the case of freight transport by ferries, for instance—the combination of ship and railroad probably increases the monopolistic profit margin.

Likewise, on a regular route, serviced by an oligopolistic group under conference arrangements, i.e., with uniform freight rates, these cannot exceed the level at which new firms would be enticed to establish services on this route or the one at which cargoes would begin to be transported by other routes. If such alternative routes do not exist, the possibility of raids by other firms will depend in essence on the relative cost positions of the firms already operating on the route on one side and of the newcomers on the other. Of course, the result is also influenced in varying degrees by the institutional barriers to entry. If a struggle does ensue, the financial superiority of one side or the other will play a major role in the outcome. If the existing firms are financially powerful, it may be that a small, low-cost firm has better entry possibilities than a large one. If, on the other hand, the already operating firms are financially weak, the opposite may be the case. Actually, a priori generalizations in this respect are hazardous; in each case particular circumstances create unique situations and the managerial ability in the entering firm may be a vital factor in many instances.

In the long run, then, the degree to which oligopoly power can be exploited is limited by the true cost advantages of group members. Moreover, the level of the freight rates charged by the oligopolists will not only be influenced by the potential competition of new entrants, but also by the structure of demand. If the buyers are "atomistic," i.e., a large number of small firms who have no special ties with the conference group, a very different result will emerge than if they are "oligopsonistic" or "monopsonistic," one or a few large firms. The latter case is quite frequent and then freight rates will be lower than in the atomistic case. This explains why in 1909 the British Royal Commission on Shipping suggested that "counter combinations on the part of merchants and shippers" might be the best answer to attempts by conferences to charge excessive freight rates.[22] In one way or another, this is precisely what users tend to do within the means at their disposal. It may be added that the regular lines are not free from competition by tramps [23] especially on routes on which the merchandise transported in one direction has the characteristics of tramp freight. In such cases a degree of competition is evidenced by the absence of a uniform rate for such cargo, even

22. Quoted in *Control of Ocean Freight Rates in Foreign Trade* (U.S. Department of Commerce, Bureau of Foreign and Domestic Commerce [Washington, D.C., 1938]), pp. 48–49.

23. This competition makes itself felt indirectly. The long-term decline in tramp freight rates has shifted investments in shipping toward regular lines which has also decreased the yield of the latter. From this Daniel Marx, Jr., concludes that "conferences have throughout their history been mainly defensive rather than aggressive cartels . . ." (*International Shipping Cartels*, pp. 242–43). This is the conclusion generally reached by economists who have made objective studies of the conference system, in spite of the frequent complaints by users and governments about the level of freight rates. See, for example, Werner Nittscher, "Das Konferenzsystem der Linienschiffahrt," in *Wirtschaftdienst Monatschrift* (Hamburg, June, 1956), p. 322.

when a conference exists. Instead an open rate will exist, which will be freely contracted for each transaction.

Thus, the freight rates of regular lines are not arrived at by perfect competition, but neither are they a pure monopoly price. And it may well be argued that their difference from the really competitive structure of tramp markets is compensated by their greater stability. The latter becomes more obvious when one considers the strong disequilibrating forces to which the international ocean freight transport market is generally subjected. Table 3 bears out the point. This table shows what happened during the first year of World War II.

TABLE 3
Voyages between the United States and the
East Coast of South America:
Indices of Limited Time-Charter Rates and Conference Rates
(August 1939 = 100)

	Time-charter rate	Conference rate
1939		
August	100	100
September	226	100
October	234	100
November	240	100
December	278	110
1940		
January	238	110
February	332	110
March	338	120
April	380	120
May	369	120
June	338	120
July	226	130

Source: *Anteproyecto de Ley de Fomento y Defensa de la Marina Mercante Nacional* (*Draft Law for the Defense and Development of the National Merchant Fleet*), prepared by the Commission to Study the Defense and Development of the Merchant Fleet (Havana: Editorial Esfuerzo, 1945), p. 28.

More recently, the outbreaks of the Korean War and the Suez conflict again were accompanied by barely a ripple in conference rates, while the rise in tramp prices was as sudden as it was violent, and costs rose about equally for both.[24]

Structure and Rates of Cuba's International Ocean Freight Market

Earlier in this chapter it was indicated that an important distinction between several markets exists in Cuba's international ocean traffic. Cuban exports are serviced primarily by tramps or by ships whose rates are governed by the tramp market. Imports, on the other hand, are mainly transported by liners; import freight rates are consequently subject to the influences of the regular line market.

We have tried to make clear the general significance of this distinction by emphasizing the major causes or economic forces involved. It now remains to apply the analysis to a description and theoretical interpretation of the actual facts of Cuba's international ocean cargo transport.

EXPORTS

In Chapter 1 it was stated that in 1956 out of a total export volume of 7,610,943 metric tons, liquid cargo amounted to 1,376,122 tons and dry cargo to 6,234,821 tons. It was mentioned further that while almost all the liquid freight went to the United States, 3,392,197 tons of the dry cargo went to that country and 2,822,624 tons to a considerable number of others.

In spite of their considerable volume, liquid cargo exports,

24. This confirms D. H. Robertson's judgment that "the liner companies are at once less sensitive to movements in market demands and more sensitive to movements in costs than the owners of tramps" (*Economic Fragments* [London: P. S. King & Sons, 1931], p. 122, quoted by Marx, *International Shipping Cartels*, p. 242).

consisting of inverted and blackstrap molasses, are relatively unimportant for Cuba's overall ocean transport economy. Some three vessels participate in this trade under the Cuban flag. We have tried to obtain detailed information on this market; not being successful in this, we must presume that its traits are broadly similar to those of the petroleum tankers' trade. Freight rates per ton are low but at least for the vessels not owned by the large oil companies,[25] subject to greater fluctuations than those of dry cargo tramps (see Chart II).

CHART II
Indices of Charter Rates for Tankers and
Dry-Cargo Freighters
(July-December 1947 = 100)

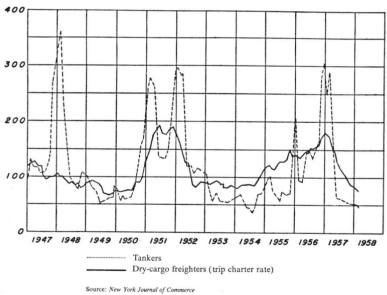

------------ Tankers
──────── Dry-cargo freighters (trip charter rate)

Source: *New York Journal of Commerce*
Computations: *Norwegian Shipping News*

25. The proportion which the oil companies own of the total of available tanker tonnage still exceeds that of the independent proprietors. But it has been calculated that by 1963 the latter should account for almost 56 per cent of the total. See the *New York Times*, October 4, 1957.

If freight rates for the export of molasses are linked to the rates for petroleum, they must be highly competitive and similarly exposed to considerable ups and downs. However, to the extent to which at least part of the vessels used belong directly to the molasses selling or exporting interests, competition becomes more questionable. If the export of molasses, particularly blackstrap, were to expand and become a large, steady, trade item, these freights might acquire considerable importance. But because the routes differ, and for other reasons, it could hardly provide petroleum tankers with return freight. It is therefore doubtful that such an expansion would act favorably on Cuba's liquid cargo freight rates, either for exports or for the fuel imports needed for economic development. As noted earlier, the normal rate for petroleum shipments oscillates between $2.00 and $2.50 per ton; it is therefore likely that the rate for molasses also lies within this range, although in practice it may also be somewhat higher.

Regarding Cuba's dry cargo exports, it was pointed out earlier that sugar represents 81 per cent of such shipments to the United States, and 91 per cent to other countries. Most of our attention has therefore to be devoted to freight rates for this product.

We do not have enough data for a detailed analysis of sugar exports to countries other than the United States. It is our impression that these freight rates normally fluctuate more violently than those of shipments to United States ports. One reason is that the demand for Cuba's sugar is more unstable in this market than in the United States. Besides, the individual shipments are larger and are usually transported in vessels that have real alternatives in the form of coal, cereals, and other bulk cargoes. Profits in boom times are probably greater than on United States–Cuban routes, but so are losses, at least on the short run, when prices are depressed. Cuban shipping concerns only supply this service in very exceptional cases.

CHART III
Indices of Trip- and Time-Charter Rates and of Raw Sugar
Freight Rates, North Coast of Cuba to Eastern Seaboard
of the United States, North of Cape Hatteras
(July–December 1947 = 100)

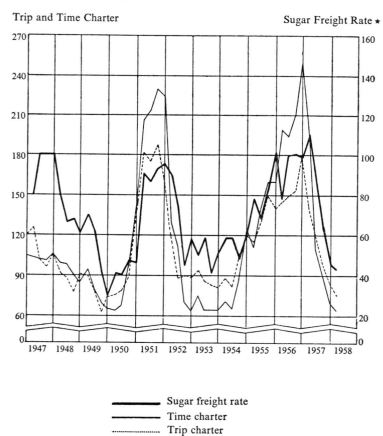

Trip and Time Charter   Sugar Freight Rate ★

——————— Sugar freight rate
——————— Time charter
·················· Trip charter

★ Sugar freight rates minus $0.20 per 100 pounds for loading and unloading.

Freight rates of sugar shipped to the United States are more
amenable to analysis since the data are more satisfactory. We
have noted already that the service is supplied by tramps,

although some exceptions to this exist, consisting mainly of small lots destined for other countries by way of trans-shipment in New York. Competition is therefore extremely vigorous. The factor that most directly determines this type of freight rate is evidently the charter rate. Chart III confirms this: The monthly average raw sugar freight rate for shipments to the United States north of Cape Hatteras closely follows the average dry cargo tramp charter rate.

What divergences exist between them are mainly accounted for by the fact that the charter rate includes also vessels of a type other than those most suitable for the Cuba–United States sugar trade. Even so, the correlation is extremely close although, presumably, the sugar freight rate is also somewhat influenced by the United States demand for Cuban sugar itself; at least it appears that frequently the freight rate rises seasonally in the months in which shipments are at their peak.

In Chart III, Cuba–United States sugar freight rates are represented by an index for shipments north of Cape Hatteras. Had we plotted another curve for shipments originating in the same Cuban ports, but destined for Gulf ports, a close correspondence between both lines would have been found. There would also, however, appear a tendency for the lines to diverge in periods of price rises and for the gap to narrow when prices fall. Thus, freight rates to the Gulf zone (southeast of the United States and Gulf of Mexico) may be somewhat more stable than those for ports north of Cape Hatteras. The interesting questions suggested by the system of rates according to zones, the demarcation of which can largely be explained by the locational structure of the United States refining industry, will have to be ignored in this study. The difference of behavior of the two series in periods of rising and declining rates respectively may perhaps be explained by changes in the bargaining power of shipping operators and sugar exporters or refiners. When the demand for shipping is high, the cost differences involved in the larger voyage can better be passed on to the buyer; but when cargo space is plentiful, operators may absorb these cost differences. Moreover, when the operators' bargaining power is high, the normal zones (which for Cuban trade are further subdivided into its northern and its southern coast) tend to splinter and a whole series of subzones are established, both according to origin and according to destination. Likewise, as market conditions change, the range of options among ports in which loading and unloading may occur under the charter widens or narrows. All this, however, must be understood to apply only when prices and costs lie within a broad normal range; in more extreme situations the exercise of bargaining power by shippers and operators will take different forms. Thus, when rates fall to a level where differences of a fraction of a point may mean losses or increases in losses, operators' resistance to further concessions may stiffen, all the more so if they use time-charter vessels and can thus reduce the size of their fleet.

It is also worth remembering that at each point in time different sugar freight rate structures by zones may emerge according to the degree to which shippers' and operators' preferences happen to coincide or to differ as to ports of embarkation and destination. Thus, if an operator has a cargo from a Gulf port to Havana, he is more likely to accept a lower rate for a sugar shipment to the Gulf area than he would be if he had no return cargo. The degree to which this willingness results in an actual freight rate reduction depends at least in part on how interested the shippers of sugar are in having their freight delivered to a port convenient to the operator. Given the economic pressure to avoid empty holds, operators will often be forced to consent to such reductions, especially in the voyage to the United States. This is a very important feature of the traffic between Cuba and the United States and one which results from the usual imbalance in time and space between the exigencies of import and export transport services. In the final analysis it is only another sign of the serious difficulties which the need to combine tramp services, required for the export trade, and regular line services, needed for imports, create for Cuban shipping concerns that can specialize in neither one nor the other, nor both. Such specialization is precluded by the lack of the regular and stable exports to the United States that would suit scheduled lines. It follows that although the rates for Cuban sugar shipped to the United States are mainly determined by quotations of the world tramp market, which always set the upper limit, they are also influenced by the availability of vessels bringing imports to Cuban ports. Thus the given presence of these ships exerts a constant pressure on rates and will tend to maintain them below the upper limit set by the world market. If, then, the supply of bottoms were suddenly increased by a so-called development program for the national merchant fleet, and if existing services were maintained, the carrying capacity of the latter would become under-utilized and it might even occur that insufficient sugar would be available to use all the available holds for the export trade.   Given the present number of vessels operating between the United States and Cuba, this possibility might come to pass if only some ten ships of no more than 5,000 tons displacement capacity each were added. The ensuing competition would clearly reduce prices until some of the present tramp operators reduced the size of their fleet or went out of business.

After this summary of the chief characteristics of Cuba's most important freight market, that for sugar, we can complete the general picture by a brief sketch of some other items. The most important one is minerals, which in 1956 amounted to 501,657 metric tons, of which only 22,052 tons went to countries other than the United States. These exports are also mainly carried on tramps at very competitive rates. However, in some cases substantial amounts are transported in railroad cars by way of the maritime ferry service.

Of significance, too, are fresh fruit and vegetable exports, primarily to the United States. A substantial proportion is transported via the ferry service, and most of the remainder goes in special refrigerated ships with regular runs between Havana and New York. This trade poses some serious problems, derived fundamentally from the demand and supply conditions for such products. This is not the place to inquire into the various causes that, in the view of domestic producers, have made the position of Cuban fruits and vegetables increasingly precarious in the United States market, particularly in New York. Although demand has risen, it has done so much more for processed (canned, preserved, etc.) fruits and vegetables than for fresh ones. Competition has become sharper, both from United States producers and from other countries. In Cuba, production costs have risen considerably. Cuban production is therefore under great pressure from both the demand and the supply side. In the absence of a detailed study there has been a tendency to impute the blame for this situation to the shortage and the high price of ocean transportation. The accusation seems groundless to us and is contradicted by the fact that the concerns offering this particular service charge rates that cover marginal, but not average, transport costs. They are thus, in a way, subsidizing the Cuban fruit and vegetable growers. It has also been alleged that with more frequent sailings exports would increase. But this argument fails to consider that vessels for the Havana–New York route need special technical features, including a minimum tonnage. A single new boat would therefore add 25 per cent to the presently available capacity, which may in some ways be insufficient during the peak season (roughly the first six months), but which is excessive during the rest of the year.

That the supply of Cuban fruits and vegetables does not respond readily to increases in sailings of the specialized vessels needed to transport such produce was shown when a temporary increase actually took place. The same tonnage was merely distributed among more ships, so that unit costs rose and the overall operating deficit increased; this finally forced rates up, although not enough to wipe out the losses. We have

here a clear case of monopoly—or quasi-monopoly, since ferries do offer a competitive alternative of sorts—not necessarily
leading to a market price above either production costs or
above the price resulting from the presence of larger numbers
of suppliers. In the case of Cuban fruits and vegetables an
objective analysis will clearly show that the opposite happened.
In spite of the quasi-monopoly power of the firm engaged in
this business, it has for a number of years chosen to transport
part of Cuba's fruit and vegetable exports to New York at rates
that did not cover the full costs of the service. Presumably an
explanation for this fact is to be found among factors akin to
those listed above under *b* when we attempted to classify the
determinants of monopolistic and oligopolistic freight rates,
i.e., the "political" consequences of higher rates. The shipping
concern will try to evade such consequences on the short run,
but will have to face them eventually, when compelled to it
by the normal businessman's reluctance to employ his resources
to less than best advantage.

The remaining export items are large in number but small
in volume and diverse in destination. Like fruits and vegetables they are therefore mostly shipped on regular liners,
except in cases like that of scrap iron, in which complete shipments can usually be made on unscheduled boats.

To sum up: Cuban exports are mostly shipped at highly competitive freight rates which preclude abnormal profits. Even
the goods shipped by way of the somewhat more monopolistic
regular lines, sometimes pay rates—fruits and vegetables to
New York are a case in point—below the costs of supplying
the service.

IMPORTS

The freight rates for crude and refined petroleum imports
have already been discussed; the remainder, dry cargo, can
be subdivided into bulk freight and packaged cargoes.

The following items are the most important bulk freight:

wheat, coal, and raw materials for fertilizer production. Over 90 per cent of Cuba's imports of these come from the United States. In 1956 this share was 96 per cent, or 425,817 tons out of 442,934. Almost all are brought by either voyage- or time-charter tramps. The latter type of contract is more frequent when the importers process the raw materials in question, as is the case with wheat milling and the transformation of mineral components into fertilizers, and when these processes are relatively free from seasonal fluctuations. Some of these processors even operate their own vessels.[26] Occasionally manufactured fertilizers, too, may be transported in full shiploads, but when smaller consignments are involved, they come on regular liners.

When we subtract bulk freight from total 1956 dry cargo imports, almost 2,100,000 metric tons remain, of which nearly two-thirds come from the United States. Most of these imports are transported on regular liners operated by concerns belonging to conferences.

Except for some fairly appreciable shipments of wood, most of the 700,000 metric tons originating outside the United States arrive on regular liners which include Cuban ports on their itineraries. A few of these routes are in the hands of only one firm, but most of them are serviced by two or more. Even though these concerns adhere to the uniform conference rates, they compete vigorously among each other by actively soliciting cargoes. Moreover the tramp operators who transport sugar or minerals from Cuba provide another source of competition

26. The advantages of this are debatable and depend, in the short run, on when the ships were bought, on the present level of freight rates, and on the market conditions for the merchandise transported or for the finished product into which such merchandise is to be transformed. If a firm is strong enough financially and administratively—operating ships requires very specialized managerial talents—it may benefit in the long run from owning its own vessels, since its freight costs may be more stable. But in any event the costs of the enterprise will become more inflexible and it may happen that in a vain endeavor to obtain internal economies, opportunities are lost to benefit from external ones.

to the regular lines since, rather than having to sail with ballast in their holds, they will make themselves available for some types of merchandise, particularly heavy ironware and European automobiles. Finally, lines with Cuban ports of call have to compete with others who, without touching Cuba, will offer trans-shipments of merchandise, destined for Cuba, in foreign ports, principally New York.

In general then, it seems certain that the freight rates for Cuban imports not originating in the United States are rather low, a conclusion that is reinforced when the cost conditions of the vessels involved are considered. Competition, indeed, is so active that the conference agreements become rather unstable and the agreed upon rate levels are frequently undercut.

Of the 700,000 tons in question, about 500,000 arrive in Havana, 100,000 in Santiago de Cuba, and some 75,000 in El Mariel. Of the remaining ports very few receive tonnage in excess of 10,000 tons.

The dry cargo from the United States that is not imported in bulk comes from over forty different ports, although New York, New Orleans, West Palm Beach, Houston, Baltimore, and San Francisco, in that order of importance, account for more than 70 per cent of the total. Atlantic Coast and Gulf ports supply over 90 per cent and the Pacific Coast the remainder.

Havana receives approximately one million tons of this total, Santiago de Cuba 90,000 to 100,000, El Mariel over 90,000, and the remainder (Matanzas, Pastelillo, Manzanillo, Cienfuegos, etc.) some 200,000. About 70 per cent of Havana's imports of this type arrive in freighters and the remaining 30 per cent come by ferries and "sea train." The port of El Mariel has succeeded in diverting considerable volume away from Havana through lower handling charges and by absorbing the overland transport costs. In an elementary analysis of the geographical distribution of Cuba's imports, the shipping sent to El Mariel may be considered to represent traffic deflected from the port of Havana, where freight handling has gradually become more difficult and expensive both on the piers and with regard to transportation to warehouses.

Dry cargo imports of non-bulk freight are mainly carried at conference freight rates. The existing conferences for traffic between Cuba and Atlantic and Gulf ports—which, as was noted before, represents over 90 per cent of Cuba's imports from the United States—are the following: the Havana Steamship Conference, the Gulf and South Atlantic Steamship Conference, the Cuban Out-Ports Conference, and the Santiago de Cuba Conference. In addition, the first two are linked by an interconference arrangement. For Cuban exports two conferences exist: the Havana–United States Atlantic and Gulf Agreement and the Santiago de Cuba Conference.

Conferences have a chairman who acts as coordinator between member firms, tries to maintain unity of action, serves as a friendly arbitrator, receives complaints on freight rates from operators and shippers, collects and supplies information, publishes rate revisions, etc.

Conference rates are either established according to merchandise "classes" or by applying a uniform rate per unit of weight or volume to a particular set of commodities. Under the latter system, each good has a rate applied exclusively to it according to weight or the hold space it occupies. When a conference uses both systems, the rates by commodity have priority over the rates by classes. The Havana Steamship Conference, for example, has rates for five merchandise classes, namely, in descending order, D 1, 1, 2, 3, and 4. But it also has rates for individual commodities, and these are what are actually applied. According to the usual practice, this conference's rates are lower for larger shipments and higher when a cargo does not reach the 20,000 pounds minimum level or when certain containers are used. The main reasons for this are obvious: documentation, supervision, and other activities which operators have to perform for each shipment, regardless of size, represent larger percentages for smaller shipments. Freight charges for trade between the United States and Cuba actually cover a broad spectrum of rates. At the time of this writing, those of the Havana Steamship Conference ranged between $17 per short ton—applicable to organic earths for instance—and $139 per ton for safety deposit boxes weighing more than 20 tons.

Conference rates for traffic between the United States and Cuba must be fixed at levels at which non-members are not tempted to enter the market and members not operating on this route do not feel impelled to try. Likewise, marginal operating members should not find the rate attractive enough to expand their present service.

The bargaining power of operators on routes between the United States and Cuba is further limited in the case of agricultural or manufactured goods imported by only a small number of merchants. Import quotas and duties on some agricultural items tend to encourage the importing wholesalers to collude, so that usually they are referred to as a "group." This describes accurately enough their oligopsonistic nature in buying ocean transport services. By acting together, a "group" controls a large enough payload to be able to negotiate on freight rates with a conference. Of course, its bargaining position is only strong if it not only controls a substantial payload, but also can count on independent shipping firms as potential carriers and competitors of the conference. Both conditions are fulfilled for some commodities imported by Cuba from the United States; freight rates then are close to—or often, and for considerable periods, below—the cost of supplying the service. Sometimes only one importing enterprise dominates in a particular field, and then the great volume of freight at its command and its monopsonistic position gives it great bargaining power, especially if, as is the case, competition exists among the suppliers of the service.[27]

In passing, it may be noted how closer study of the structure and behavior of Cuban markets for diverse goods and services makes them appear increasingly oligopolistic. Almost all production and distribution is in a few hands—pure oligopoly—or in many but with a few dominant firms—partial oligopoly. The best proof of this is the prevalence of advertising and other outlays designed to stimulate sales, which is the usual manifestation of imperfect competition. The remaining islands of open competition become gradually submerged; to this inexorable process tariff privileges and other interventionist and protectionist devices are major contributors. It is debatable how much these policies impinge on price levels, but it seems reasonable to suppose that the proliferation of monopolies creates a series of bilateral oligopoly situations. In these, some price rises may be avoided and nevertheless profit levels may remain attractive if increasing efficiency constantly acts to lower costs. Freight rates for rice imports from Gulf ports seem to be a notable example of this. During the last ten years these rates have hardly been raised; certainly not as much as loading and unloading costs have risen. All attempts by operators to do so have been effectively blocked by the concerted action of the users who have banded together as an oligop-

27. We may also point out that a decisive factor in making competition imperfect between many otherwise independent producers or consumers is the concentration of the export as well as the import trade in a particular commodity in one principal or gateway port. If the output of a large number of independent suppliers is channelled through a small number of middlemen into the main port of embarkation and is received by an equally small number of buyers in the port of destination, it will reach the consumers only after a fairly extensive process of distribution. The shipper then faces users whose monopoly power does not only derive from being a "group," but also from the existence of principal ports. On the question of gateway ports see August Lösch, *The Economics of Location* (New Haven: Yale University Press, 1954), pp. 187 ff.

sonistic group.[28] This would at least be one explanation of
why the agreement between the rice transporting lines does
not just stipulate a common rate; a much closer collaboration
exists, to the point where sailings and tonnages are divided
among them. The pool thus formed eliminates a major portion
of the excess capacity that would otherwise exist, and by lowering unit costs provides members with a given level of profits
even though freights have remained almost constant in the
face of generally rising costs.

Of course, the user's oligopsonistic power in international
maritime freight service does not exist merely on the Cuban
importer's side, where a simple counting of the dominant firms
or brands would suffice to confirm it. It is also present among
associations of groups, including groups in imperfectly competitive markets that fall under Chamberlin's "large number"
case. Indeed, most import categories are dominated by a few
pace-setting firms. But even exports are not exempt from
this tendency; both those shipped by regular liners, such as
fresh fruits and vegetables, and those using the very competitive tramp service, like sugar, are increasingly in the hands
of oligopsonistic shippers who constantly apply what counter-
pressure they may against ship operators' groups.

One further aspect of the freight market structure deserves
mention, namely, the various degrees of service differentiation
on routes with different economic characteristics. An illustrative
basis for discussion is provided by the New York–Havana route
on the one hand and that from southeastern seaboard ports
to Havana on the other.

On the first of these, the degree of homogeneity of the
service rendered by regularly scheduled lines is attested to by

28. These relations between oligopolists and oligopsonists can be fitted
into the framework of John K. Galbraith's theory of countervailing power.
See his *American Capitalism—The Concept of Countervailing Power*
(Boston: Houghton Mifflin, 1952).

the fact that all sailings to New York occur on the same day, Friday. The practical reason for this is that each company tries to have as many weekdays as possible to solicit freight that can be embarked without having to resort to costly weekend loading operations. The economic yield of vessels is increased by this procedure. But in the light of these facts it seems quite justified to classify the firms servicing this route as belonging to Triffin's [29] "homogeneous competition" category. This is the case in which small price (rate) variations—or rather, those strictly necessary to offset some remaining product differentiation (personal relations between shippers and operators, better piers, etc.)—would be decisive in altering the balance between the various lines working this route. It would actually be enough for one firm to reduce its freight rate fractionally to attract all the freight it could possibly carry, if the other lines maintained their prices unchanged. Similarly, only limitations in the carrying capacity of its competitors would prevent it from losing all its customers if it alone raised its rates even slightly.

By way of contrast, schedules are less rigid on the route between the southeastern coasts of the United States and Havana, and sailings are not concentrated on one day of the week. The two lines servicing this route work under conditions of "heterogeneous competition," which really amounts to imperfect or monopolitistic competition. In this case a rate reduction by line A would divert part, but not all, of line B's cargoes, even if A had enough capacity to take over the route completely.

The inference is therefore permissible and is confirmed in practice that when the product (service) is as undifferentiated as in the case of the New York–Havana route, the maintenance of a common price (rate) policy will require energetic meas-

29. Robert Triffin, *Monopolistic Competition and General Equilibrium Theory* (Cambridge, Mass.: Harvard University Press, 1949), p. 103.

ures and constant vigilance and persuasion by the management of the conference. Only thus, and by taking account of all possible relevant facts on traffic and on the relative position of each conference member, will it be possible to maintain the cohesion and uniformity of behavior which, as we have shown, can so easily be broken. If, on the other hand, service differentiation is greater, particular rate levels are less important as tools of competition. Conference rules can then be applied more flexibly, the degree of tolerance varying with that of differentiation.

We conclude that the assertion made at the beginning of this chapter was justified. Cuba's international freight rates are truly competitive, especially as far as exports are concerned. For imports we saw that the substantial proportion of the total that is liquid cargo (fuels) has its freight rates determined in the open international market. Moreover, we saw that an important part of the dry cargo imports is shipped in bulk at the extremely competitive tramp rates. And because of the particular market conditions described, we saw that even the freight imported on regular liners cannot be forced to pay excessive, monopolistic rates.

Although rates are not particularly attractive, Cuba is serv-

TABLE 4

Number of Vessels over 1000 Tons Entering Havana Annually
under Foreign Flags, 1952–1956

Flag	1952	1953	1954	1955	1956
United States	333	309	202	172	177
Norway	175	193	177	202	236
Honduras	103	81	72	65	71
Germany	77	168	172	169	134
Spain	76	86	92	86	105
Great Britain	73	70	67	60	89
Panama	49	71	97	81	62
Others	324	409	461	637	522
Total	1210	1387	1340	1472	1396

Source: Capitanía of the Port of Havana.

iced by a large number of freighters. Table 4 shows the number
of foreign cargo ships of more than one thousand tons that
entered Havana between 1952 and 1956.

Even more telling than Table 4, which excludes vessels
below 1000 tons and all Cuban ships, are the following figures:
The total number of dry hold ships and ferries entering Havana
in 1956 (excluding yachts, tugs, etc.) from abroad was 2,500;
their net registry was 5,658,986 tons. They brought 1,860,062
metric tons of dry cargo, or 3,798,924 tons less than their carrying capacity would have permitted.[30] This indicates that many
of the ships coming directly to Havana are under-utilized and
that many others touch this city as part of voyages which
include many other ports of call.[31] If we subtracted the 288
ships that bring more freight than their net registry capacity
indicates, the remaining imbalance between carrying capacity
and merchandise disembarked would be even greater. It is
true that a compensating adjustment would then have to be
made to exclude the passenger vessels whose cargo carrying
capacity is smaller than their net registry, but even then the
overall imbalance would not be seriously modified.

This idle carrying capacity again proves a thesis stated
above: Havana, which because of its importance can here be
made to stand for all Cuban ports, is excellently attended by
freighters, mainly regular liners, available for carrying imports.
But idle carrying capacity also implies relatively high costs
for supplying the service, as does the need to make port to
deliver only small quantities of freight. And in this we have
one more cause that must be added to those already indicated
of why freight rates must be high enough to permit continuation of the service.

Thus we can now incorporate into our conclusion another
assertion made at the beginning of this chapter, namely that

30. These figures were compiled from *El Avisador*.
31. This bears out what was said about the market being spatially
diffuse.

Cuba's sea-going transport services are very good indeed. This finding coincides with that of Merwin L. Bohan, who, in his *Investment in Cuba,* stressed that Cuba has excellent maritime services attended by some thirty shipping concerns.[32] Beyond some descriptive details, the author does not add much to justify this judgment, but our preceding analysis bears him out fully.

32. [Merwin L. Bohan], *Investment in Cuba* (U.S. Department of Commerce, Washington, D.C., 1956), p. 113.

3

THE COSTS OF CUBA'S INTERNATIONAL
MARITIME CARGO SERVICES

THE PRESENT CHAPTER may in some respects be regarded as the central part of our study, because the data and analysis which it contains point up the basic elements needed to understand the level of maritime freight rates charged in Cuba's export and import trade. Furthermore, they supply the information necessary to estimate the effects of these rates on Cuba's international balance of payments and the consequences which the development of a national merchant fleet would have on the foreign balance. The analysis of the cost composition of the service under study is therefore preceded by the chapter on the freight rate market structure, and is followed in turn by Chapter 4, in which an approximate estimate of the impact of freight payments on Cuba's international accounts will be attempted. This procedure will meet the dual purpose of broadly sketching the structure and functioning of Cuba's international freight transport market and, more restrictedly, of describing and throwing light on the true meaning of maritime freights for the country's balance of payments and for its national income. It will be our endeavor to clear up a number of misunderstandings and mistakes which have become common through a superficial consideration of these matters.

Regarding method, it may be noted that in this chapter the same procedure as in the preceding one will be followed: First the nature and characteristics of maritime freight transport costs in general will be outlined briefly and then the relevant data for Cuba will be introduced.

General Considerations

To the economist the study of maritime freight transport costs presents a number of difficulties resulting from some complications which make the shipping enterprise something very special. The traditional theory of the firm—the Marshallian one for example—is normally presented in non-spatial terms; but when it comes to producing transport service, distance acquires a crucial role. It is the element from which both the demand for, and the supply of, the service originate. However, although there are many ways to overcome distance and to reach a destination, only one of them will be the most efficient. Thus arises the typical problem of transportation economics: to select the most advantageous routes with respect to the income derivable from a given cargo. On the other hand, the moving of the cargo depends on the vehicle (vessel) or on the technical facilities needed for the different kinds of service. Their variety again results from differences among users, types of freight, etc., and each of these factors in turn has its own influence on the capacity, speed, reliability, and safety—to mention only a few—of the service.

Traditional concepts of economic theory are certainly excellent starting points for the logical arrangement of thought, provided that in addition the special problems which the analysis of the particular economic activity requires are also considered. Thus, in the matter of the costs of shipping firms, the basic distinction between fixed and variable costs that is normal in the theory of the firm is in principle applicable. It is, however, extremely difficult to establish a sharp and generally valid distinction between the two types of costs.

Using a simple definition, we would call fixed costs those

which do not depend on the volume of production at a given moment, while, on the other hand, variable costs are those that depend on it and that therefore fluctuate with any increase or decrease of traffic. Certainly the technical nature of a productive factor is less important than are the contractual conditions under which the firm has gained command over it. The length of time for which equipment is being used is one of the most strategic determinants of exactly which costs can be regarded as fixed and which as variable. This statement is generally valid, but quite specially so for the shipping enterprise. Proof of it lies in the fact that one and the same operator may be working with self-owned as well as chartered vessels. The ships which are the firm's property assume the character of fixed costs to a much higher degree than those working on time charter, and the shorter the charter period, the more they approach the concept of variable costs. The extreme case of this will be that of a boat chartered for just one voyage, either for a round trip or only a segment of a voyage, as sometimes happens when an established shipping organization needs to supplement its normal capacity. It can therefore be concluded that there is nothing absolute about the fixity or variability of costs incurred by operating equipment.

Another difficulty which makes the determination of costs of a maritime enterprise complicated arises from its operating on more than one route. From the possibility of transferring some of the vessels from one route to another—to mention just one of the many possible transfers of productive resources—arise alternative possibilities of defining the equipment costs as fixed or variable.

Another difficulty in this regard springs from the variety of goods to be transported. For example: Should the additional handling costs caused by the need of certain cargoes for special facilities, such as refrigeration, be considered as variable or fixed? If the costs of such installations have been incurred for the specific purpose of increasing the volume of special cargo—and thereby of total freight—then they must be considered as variable. However, if the freight which was the reason for the investment does not materialize, such costs will have to be considered fixed.

The shipping enterprise can be compared to a multiple-product firm in which the analysis of costs is complicated by the mutual interdependence of the various product lines. Normally, expansion in one department affects, either by checking or by promoting, the production of other goods or services. The more routes a company covers, the larger the number and variety of its vessels, and the greater the range of the merchandise they have to transport, especially if these vary between incoming and outgoing voyages, the more complex does the issue become. Only by treating a maritime enterprise with multiple routes, ships, and types of cargo like a firm with several plants, each specializing in one article, could the calculation of fixed, variable, and marginal costs—the last often being the most interesting—be simplified. Even simpler would be the hypothetical case of a shipper serving a single route with only one self-owned vessel which carries the same type of freight outbound and homebound, or merely carries ballast on one voyage. In such a case the genuine fixed costs consist of the organizational overhead and those of the boat itself and its crew, insurance, maintenance, etc. Only the expenses incurred through the loading and unloading of larger or smaller cargoes would be variable. On the other hand, in tramp shipping the greatest part of costs is variable. This explains why Koopmans has been able to stress the importance of marginal costs in the economy of tramps.[1]

A simplification in common usage is to base the differentia-

1. Tjalling C. Koopmans, "Optimum Utilization of the Transportation System" (Report of the Washington Meeting of the Econometric Society held in conjunction with the International Statistical Conferences, September 6–18, 1947), *Econometrica*, XVII, Supplement (July, 1949), 144.

tion between fixed and variable costs on the following assumption: (1) Service is on one given route with a constant number of voyages, and (2) the only variable factor is the amount of freight transported on this route. This means in fact that the only variable costs are those connected with the difference in quantity of tonnage transported.

Thus Grossman,[2] according to this scheme, groups fixed costs under the heading which we call *Costs of the vessel* and under *Costs of the voyage* (also called cargo and ports costs) the variable expenses, although with certain qualifications that will be discussed below. As an illustration he offers a table, reconstructed here as Table 5, based on data from the Maritime Administration of the United States, for a given vessel and voyage.[3] The data in Table 5 will help us to get an approximate idea of the relative importance of fixed and variable costs in the total service cost in ocean transportation. Naturally the items under *Costs of the vessel* do not include all the fixed costs of a shipping enterprise. Such important items as managerial and administrative expenses and depreciation of its vessels have been left out. On the other hand, neither the fixed costs of the vessel, nor the variable character of voyage expenses can be sharply defined. Overtime work may make wages quite variable, for example. The same applies to fuel, since on a given ship its consumption may be altered by a number of factors.

Similarly, although the "costs of the voyage," i.e., those of

2. William L. Grossman, *Ocean Freight Rates,* pp. 54 ff.
3. The voyage he had in mind must have been an extremely long one, which could partly explain the high percentage of the total operating costs represented by the payroll. In Chapter 4 we shall show in detail the relation between costs of the crew and total costs of a voyage according to its duration. The reason will be given why in the traffic between Cuba and the United States the remuneration of the crew is of much smaller importance than could be concluded from Table 5. It is in fact only a fraction of total costs or of gross freights. It must also be remembered that wages of American sailors are fantastically high.

TABLE 5
Cost Distribution in Ocean Transportation

Costs of the vessel:		
Crew payroll		28.5
Payroll taxes		0.9
Social benefits		1.3
Maintenance		2.4
Provisions, supply, and equipment		2.3
Other maintenance expenses		2.6
Fuel		10.9
Repairs		3.1
Insurance (hull and engines)		2.6
Other insurance		4.4
Other expenses of the vessel		0.3
Total expenses of the vessel		59.3
Costs of the voyage:		
Port charges		
Agencies	1.3	
Docking	3.4	
Other port charges	5.6	
		10.3
Cargo costs		
Stowage	19.2	
Other cargo expenses	7.7	
		26.9
Commissions for freight		0.5
Other voyage expenses		3.0
Total voyage expenses		40.7

Total operating costs of the ship: 100.00

Source: Based on William L. Grossman, *Ocean Freight Rates* (Cambridge, Md.; copyright 1956 by Cornell Maritime Press), p. 54.

freight and port charges, are to a great extent variable, they contain, or at least may contain, some elements of fixed costs. Pier-use charges and pilot fees, for example, are as a rule independent of cargo tonnage. Another variable item that can switch over to fixed costs, especially in the case of important maritime firms, is the consignation of the vessel, when this function is transferred to an office belonging to the shipping firm instead of an independent agency.

Costs and Size of the Maritime Enterprise
and Industry

The relationship between costs and the so-called economies of scale or size in enterprise and industry is well known.[4] It is the tendency of these economies to check the growth of certain costs in proportion to and within certain limits of the level of production growth. The influence of economies of scale upon the costs of the maritime business is evident; cargo transport service clearly has the tendency to operate like an industry with decreasing costs. A brief analysis will bear this out.

The presence of these economies in the overhead of management and administration of a shipping concern is worth noting. Clearly the complex character of the maritime business requires highly developed managerial abilities. The reason for the complexity of this activity can be found in the unstable character of ocean traffic with its exposure to constant and violent fluctuations, rapid change in prospects, and unique difficulties in correctly forecasting future developments. The need for outstanding capability grows when a shipping enterprise without "extra-market" protection operates in an area where it has to compete with firms of other nationalities which enjoy the advantage of favorable treatment and protection by their governments. If such a maritime business has succeeded in winning for itself a stable position in the market, the capacity of its managers may be taken for granted. Most probably this capacity will bear even better fruit with an increase, within certain limits, in the size and importance of the firm.

To establish new routes and thereby rationalize operations, aiming in particular at equilibrium between outward- and homeward-bound freights, and also compensating seasonal fluc-

---

4. E. A. G. Robinson's work, *The Structure of Competitive Industry* ("The Cambridge Economic Handbooks" [London: Nisbet & Co., 1952]) can be recommended for obtaining a general knowledge of the importance of economies of scale.

tuations of different kinds of cargo, is one way of making the business grow. Naturally, these results cannot always be obtained through the opening of new routes, and, therefore, the desire to attain them may sometimes be either an incentive or a deterrent to expansion along this line.

Expanding within a given route carries with it the possibility of reducing costs through the absorption by the firm of certain services originally assigned to outsiders. The decision whether to replace an independent agency by one's own office will be made only after a thorough investigation of whether the costs of such an office will be less than the commissions paid to the agent. Prospects of tonnage to be handled and the amount of the agent's commissions must therefore shape this decision.

The possibility of operating a larger vessel can also increase economies of scale. This possibility, however, requires not only the necessary volume of freight, but also adequate port facilities. Once these two requirements are met, there is no doubt that within certain limits the costs of transport per unit decrease as the vessel's capacity rises. In this context, capacity may mean not merely the size of the vessel, but all those elements which, apart from its size, make it "technically" capable of transporting freight: speed of crossing, performance of the loading and unloading equipment, distribution of hold and hatches, etc.

Further economies of an expanding maritime business can stem from integration of port facilities into one and the same enterprise. If the tonnage to be handled has reached a substantial volume and thus guarantees a certain minimum of activity, it will be profitable to own a terminal. Even when a port terminal is not owned or held under a long-term lease, the quantity and volume of cargo can bring about cost reductions in the handling process.

It can be inferred from these and other examples that economies of scale tend to a certain extent to transform variable costs, or those that possess some elements of variability, into fixed costs. This transformation has a marked impact on the equilibrium of the firm and on its profit maximization. It will increase net income in times of prosperity, but will reduce the flexibility needed for the adaption of expenses to periods of depression, unless a firm becomes so strong that its position of leadership is assured against its competitors.

Quite apart from the internal economies of the individual shipping concern, notice must be taken of the external economies made possible through an increase of the economic importance of the whole industry for geographical or other reasons. If complementary activities are achieving a higher degree of specialization and efficiency, the efficiency of the maritime enterprise itself will also increase. And this refers not only to advantages gained from private efforts, but also to those which result from official initiative.

There exists a wide range of possibilities for attaining external cost economies. Among them the vessel's supply, provisioning, and repair services may be singled out. The advantages for the operator of a growing number of ports with adequate facilities for these services are evident. To have fuel available, for example, permits a better utilization of cargo capacity, while adequate docks help to maintain the vessel in good operating shape. It goes without saying that this is true only if such services are being offered at attractive conditions. The improvement of port facilities, for example, by means of a dredging machine, which allows bigger boats the use of the port, is an instance of the many benefits that can be derived from timely action by governments.

Sales Costs in the Shipping Business

In theory as well as practice the distinctive cost features of firms operating in imperfectly competitive markets are well known. Such enterprises have to add the so-called sales costs [5] to their actual production costs. Theoretically, under perfect competitive conditions, the only costs possible are those of production; in monopolistic structures, however, costs or expenses incurred for sales promotion acquire special importance. While it is not possible in fully competitive markets to influence demand in favor of a particular enterprise when many are offering a homogeneous product, this would be feasible in imperfect markets by increasing expenses for sales promotion and thus shifting the demand curve in favor of the goods or services in question. This modification of the curve can be reached either by creating the desire for the product (or service), or by making its existence known. Once the demand has been created or the existence of the particular product or service has been publicized, further spending is necessary for maintaining and increasing sales. Intensive advertising and publicity efforts of many kinds have to be undertaken to achieve close relations with the customers.

To create demand in the maritime freight transport business —not in passenger service—such advertising would seem superfluous even in monopolistic routes; the demand for transport service is derived demand not susceptible to direct manipulation. If a product is in demand, means for its transportation will be demanded, not the reverse. Concerning the second aspect, information about the existence of a particular cargo service, there is definitely a limit to the influence that can be exerted by individual shipping concerns in the use of publicity and promotional campaigns. As a rule, normal users know about existing freight services; advertising is therefore usually restricted to the announcement of *new* services, or of changes in schedules, frequency, and regularity of sailings. There are exceptions, of course, in cases in which for reasons of competition

5. See Edward Hastings Chamberlin, *The Theory of Monopolistic Competition, a Reorientation of the Theory of Value* (6th ed., Cambridge, Mass.: Harvard University Press, 1950).

a firm is particularly interested in publicizing an important event, like a modification of its freight rates on routes normally renowned for their stability.[6] These cases, however, are not frequent and for the rest the repeated advertising of permanent services might at best attract only an occasional user, who as a rule is economically unimportant. The important ones know both the shipping concerns and the conditions under which their services are available.

Consequently, expenses for sales promotion through publicity are usually negligible for lines exclusively devoted to the transportation of freight, somewhat higher for lines with mixed cargo and passenger services, and much larger for lines dedicated mainly or wholly to passenger transportation.[7] However, even though publicity costs in the maritime cargo business are extremely small in comparison to those of other producers of goods or services in imperfect markets, the monopolistic structure of vast sectors of ocean transport undoubtedly originates other expenditures that should also be regarded as belonging to sales promotional costs in the sense used here. Such costs are basically linked with the soliciting of cargo and through them there is an attempt to promote and maintain congenial and close relations between the shipping operator and his customers.

It is very difficult to analyze the impact of soliciting expenses

6. The latter necessarily means a rupture of the agreement (for example, a conference) by which uniform freight rates have been agreed upon, i.e., that the most important variable factor, previously controlled jointly by all firms, is now being handled individually. There would be no practical reason whatever for an advertisement by any particular firm of controlled and uniform freight rates.

7. Actually the publicity programs of shipping lines are usually unconnected with their normal business. Rather, they are carried out because of the peculiar slavish submission to the thesis of the value of advertising that is implicitly accepted in modern times by most businesses of a certain size. It also is a convenient reaction to the need—imagined or real—of engaging in "extra-market" activities or of responding occasionally to those of competitors.

on the progress of the maritime business. It depends on the kind of traffic, i.e., the kind of merchandise to be transported on particular routes, the competition to be reckoned with, and the characteristics and economic position of each firm; in short, on a large and complex set of factors which make a generalized appraisal impossible. In any event, the acquisition of a given volume of cargo by no means always depends directly on the "soliciting" effort, just as publicity costs do not always correspond to sales results. The quality of service and facilities offered, the standing of the maritime enterprise and the confidence it inspires, the many types of links that may exist between its directors and the customers, in short, sympathy and friendship between them, all influence the acquisition of cargo. A *new* firm, entering an existent market, needs publicity and soliciting work to acquire freight. Once a certain share of total freight available has been acquired, however, promotional work in the proper sense of the word decreases, while the other aspects of acquisition of cargo grow in importance. For instance, if the shipping firm were to be sold and carried on under new management, the volume of business would change —decrease or increase—in spite of the same amount of soliciting work.

In summary, it is obvious that expenditure for sales promotion varies from firm to firm, but even so, the principle of costs decreasing as size increases is also valid for this type of expenditure in the maritime operation. Actual experience shows, however, that soliciting of cargo and publicity do not constitute any considerable share of the total overhead or even of the income derived from freights and may not exceed 1 per cent of either total.

Finally, it should be stressed that since expenses for sales promotion, or "connections," as Chamberlin calls them, are not important in the maritime business, they have much less influence on the total cost of the service than is usual in other lines of production. The implications of this in relation to the price charged for the service (freight rates) is obvious.

The Costs of Cuban Maritime Transport

We have so far considered the nature of ocean transport costs in general, without going into detail about their classification and behavior. To apply our theory to the facts of Cuba's international maritime cargo transport we will start with a number of different assumptions and gradually approach real conditions.

SOME SIMPLE MODELS

a) The simplest case. For Cuba's international ocean traffic the simplest hypothetical case might be the following: a shipping concern operating a single, wholly owned vessel, carrying a bulk load of raw sugar, shipped from a port on Cuba's north coast, for example, Nuevitas, to a United States port north of Cape Hatteras—say, Baltimore—and returning in ballast. Having selected these facts, we shall have to elaborate on some of them, particularly on the characteristics of the ship used for the service. For our purpose we choose a vessel of 3850 tons dead weight with a loading capacity of 3500 Spanish long tons, with two identical holds, each of them attended by two hands, and a third hold of half the capacity of one of the previous ones, attended by one hand; speed, thirteen knots; fuel consumption, eight tons of diesel oil (at $33 per ton) per sailing day and two tons per day in port. Let us further suppose that the vessel is of modern construction, that it cost $1,000,000, and that its depreciation period is about twenty years. An interest charge of 6 per cent of the cost price will be imputed to fixed costs. This interest charge should be adjusted downward in the course of time, but we will not do so because such a reduction might well be outweighed by the increase over the years of other items, like maintenance, repairs, and dry dock.

These data, in turn, permit us to establish the time needed for stowage, unloading, and sailing, and thus to obtain an estimate of the duration of a complete voyage:

Loading in Nuevitas. A "loading job" [8] of sugar in Nuevitas consists of 2400 bags per day and hand. Our boat with its five available hands can therefore stow approximately 12,000 bags daily. The time needed for the loading of the total cargo would be two and a half days.

Unloading in Baltimore. Unloading takes less time than loading because the work is easier and, besides, the slings in the United States hold eight to nine bags against five in Cuba. Unloading, therefore, takes only two days.

Sailing from Nuevitas to Baltimore and back. Since the distance between Nuevitas and Baltimore is 1190 nautical miles, the boat, at 13 miles an hour, or 312 miles a day, would cover the distance in not quite four days. The return trip would require, on the average, the same time, because although the vessel in ballast sails faster in summer, it might lose speed in winter, when rough seas force the propeller out of the water. Consequently, sailing time for the round trip has to be estimated at eight days.

Lost time. Saturday's and Sunday's loading and unloading operations are the reason why, without being overly conservative, one must reckon with about one and a half additional days for each round trip. Furthermore, rough sailing weather, rain in port, and other incidents like strikes, etc., frequently cause considerable delay. All in all, therefore, a minimum of fourteen days is required for the round trip, i.e., two and a half for stowing, two for unloading, eight for sailing, and one and a half lost for other reasons. Consequently, taking into account the manifold imponderables which tend to affect ocean traffic, as for example the time lost in dry dock, a maximum of twenty-five round trips per year can be accomplished by our hypothetical ship.

After thus listing most of the details that make possible the

8. By "loading job" we mean the maximum number of bags that a gang of stowers assigned to one "hand" can load in an eight-hour workday.

calculation which interests us, we present Table 6 to show the costs of transporting the raw sugar from Nuevitas to Baltimore, returning in ballast. To make the picture as clear as possible, we shall express the costs per year, per voyage, per ton, and per hundred pounds, in other words in the various most significant measurements. The calculation per hundred pounds allows a direct comparison between costs and freight rates,

TABLE 6
Model of Cost of Transport of Raw Sugar, Nuevitas–Baltimore, Return Trip in Ballast
(25 round trips per year) *

| Item | Costs per: | | | |
	Year	Voyage	Ton of 2240 lbs.	100 lbs.
Costs of the vessel:				
Depreciation, 5%	$ 50,000	$ 2,000	$ .5714	$ .0254
Interest, 6%	60,000	2,400	.6857	.0306
Insurance, 4.5%	45,000	1,800	.5143	.0230
Payroll	60,000	2,500	.6857	.0306
Extra crew	6,250	250	.0714	.0032
Provisions	18,000	720	.2057	.0092
Fuel	60,000	2,400	.6857	.0306
Maintenance	12,000	480	.1371	.0061
Repairs	12,000	480	.1371	.0061
Dry dock	15,000	600	.1714	.0077
Total	$338,250	$13,530	$3.8655	$0.1725
Costs of the voyage:				
Port charges:				
Cuba (Nuevitas)	$ 16,875	$ 675	$ .1929	$ .0086
U.S.A. (Baltimore)	18,750	750	.2143	.0096
Wages:				
Loading (Nuevitas)	157,500	6,300	1.8000	.0804
Unloading (Baltimore)	215,250	8,610	2.4600	.1098
Other expenses	12,500	500	.1429	.0064
Commissions, 2.5%	19,465	780	.2225	.0099
Total	$440,340	$17,615	$5.0326	$0.2247
Total transport cost	$778,590	$31,145	$8.8981	$0.3972

* This figure allows for an annual transport of 87,500 long tons of raw sugar in bags.

which in market usage are quoted per hundred pounds, and is therefore particularly interesting.

In Table 6 the various components of total transport costs have been grouped in a manner similar to Grossman's procedure in Table 5, adding certain items and omitting details of others. Thus, under *Costs of the vessel* we have included dry dock, while under *Costs of the voyage* port charges have not been itemized because of their numerous components, which include pier charges, harbor pilot fees, mooring and unmooring, agency, radio-telephone service, launch, mooring and unmooring of lines and cables, transportation of stevedores, automobile service, etc.

A vital omission in the cost calculation of Table 6 is the managerial and administrative costs of the maritime firm that renders the service. We will be on the safe side if we assume that this item will mean an additional 5 per cent of the total costs, or $40,000 yearly, i.e., more or less two cents per hundred pounds of raw sugar. On the other hand, not only the cost of the capital invested in the ship itself, but also the investment required by establishing and operating the enterprise should be taken into account.

b) A less simple case. To approach reality a little more closely, we shall continue by considering another case, somewhat more complex than the first. We will make the same assumptions about ports, vessel, and the merchandise to be exported, i.e. raw sugar, but will introduce a difference from the previous case on the return trip from Baltimore to Nuevitas, which this time will not be in ballast, but with a cargo of fertilizer in bags.

In this case the round trip will take twenty-four instead of fourteen days. The ten additional days are accounted for by three days of stowage in Baltimore, five of unloading in Nuevitas, and an extension of lost time from one and a half to three and a half days. Accordingly, the number of round trips to be performed yearly by the boat will be reduced to fifteen.

There should be no doubt about the basic assumption of this case. It is that the vessel always carries sugar on the outbound and fertilizer on the homeward-bound voyage and that sailings take place steadily and continuously between the two ports in question. Only then will the calculated costs really correspond to the data of our model. Later we will point out to what extent real conditions differ from this simplification. The

Duration of the voyage	*Days*
Loading of sugar in Nuevitas	2.5
Sailing time to Baltimore	4.0
Unloading of sugar in Baltimore	2.0
Loading of fertilizer in Baltimore	3.0
Sailing time to Nuevitas	4.0
Unloading of fertilizer in Nuevitas	5.0
Lost time	3.5
Total	24.0

duration of the round trip can now be calculated. The transport of raw sugar requires ten of the total of twenty-four days of the voyage (including one and a half additional days), while the remaining fourteen days are used up by transporting the return load of fertilizer.

To simplify the listing of the costs of the round trip, let us suppose that the shipper has contracted the transport of fertilizer under the customary condition for this kind of goods, called "free of stowage and unloading," or f.i.o. (free in and out). This means that the freight rate does not include loading and unloading charges. Concerning the cargo of raw sugar, we can use the data of Table 6 with only the adjustment that the annual crossings will number fifteen voyages of ten days each for the transport of sugar. The annually transported load will then be 52,500 Spanish long tons instead of 87,500, which was the annual figure calculated for a vessel carrying only sugar and returning in ballast.

TABLE 7
Model of Cost of Transport, Nuevitas–Baltimore,
Raw Sugar Outbound, Fertilizer Homeward Bound
(15 annual round trips) *

Item	Costs per:			
	Year	Voyage	Ton of 2240 lbs.	100 lbs.
Sugar				
Costs of vessel	$136,418	$ 8,095	$ 2.5985	$ .1159
Costs of voyage	256,350	17,090	4.8826	.2180
Total	$392,768	$25,185	$ 7.4811	$0.3339
Fertilizer				
Costs of vessel	$186,831	$12,455	$ 3.5487	†
Costs of voyage	13,500	900	9.2571	†
Total	$200,331	$13,355	$12.8058	†

* This figure allows for an annual transport of 52,500 long tons of raw sugar in bags.

† Not shown because freight rates for fertilizer are not usually quoted on this basis.

In this case the transport costs of sugar have decreased by about six cents per hundred pounds, or approximately $1.40 per long ton, from their level when we assumed that the vessel returns in ballast. Clearly, this somewhat less simplified second example yields a more favorable case than the first, more simplified, assumption, if the freight rate for the cargo of fertilizer covers the f.i.o. costs or at least does not cause losses that offset the advantages in the sugar cargo. In actual fact, however, it is practically impossible for a shipper to succeed in coordinating his service to such an extent that he really always has the outgoing and return freight available, as was assumed above. One can be sure that even if it were feasible to have a steady supply of sugar freight from Nuevitas to Baltimore, it would be pure chance to obtain the fertilizer as a return freight. And to have the quantity required to avoid return voyages in ballast constantly available would be most improbable. The same, of course, would apply to the sugar cargo, if the fertilizer were regularly available. To approach gradually closer to reality, therefore, we must next outline the assumptions and data of a more complex, but more realistic, case.

c) *A more complex, but more realistic case.* We shall now examine a round trip starting in Nuevitas with a complete cargo of raw sugar for Baltimore. Fertilizer in bags, destination

TABLE 8
Model of Cost of Transport of Sugar, Nuevitas–Baltimore,
Returning with Fertilizer to Havana
and Sailing in Ballast to Nuevitas
(14 annual round trips)

Item	Costs per:			
	Year	Voyage	Ton of 2240 lbs.	100 lbs.
Sugar				
Costs of vessel	$130,200	$ 9,300	$2.6571	$ .1188
Costs of voyage	241,500	17,250	4.9256	.2200
Total	$371,700	$26,550	$7.5827	$0.3388
Fertilizer				
Costs of vessel	$172,480	$12,320	$3.5200	°
Costs of voyage	16,100	1,150	.3286	°
Total	$188,580	$13,470	$3.8486	°

° Not shown because freight rates for fertilizer are not usually quoted on this basis.

Havana, will be taken on there, and from Havana the vessel will return to Nuevitas in ballast. The variation from the previous case is based on the unloading of the fertilizer in Havana instead of Nuevitas. The specifications of the ship remain unchanged. The round trip will take twenty-five days, i.e., one day more than in the previous model. This difference corresponds approximately to the sailing time Havana–Nuevitas. The number of annual voyages will consequently be fourteen instead of the fifteen which the vessel was able to perform when it returned with the cargo of fertilizer directly to Nuevitas. The costs of transport of sugar are slightly higher because port charges in Nuevitas, which in hypothesis *b* were allocated to sugar and fertilizer in equal proportions, now have to be charged wholly to sugar. Sailing in ballast from Havana to Nuevitas likewise causes a slight increase of the transport costs of the fertilizer. A comparison of costs of the transport of sugar in hypothesis *c* with those of case *a* shows, however, that *c* is generally preferable to *a*.

Hypothetical case *b* yields the minimum cost combination, but it has already been pointed out that an adequate freight supply for its realization is practically impossible. Supposition *c* will therefore probably offer the most realistic alternative.

Although this last hypothetical case approaches reality more closely than the other two, it should be stressed that it is still an abstraction. Reality is much more complex still, which leads us to the following considerations.

THE COMPLEXITY OF THE REAL WORLD

The fact that in Cuba export and import cargoes differ greatly in composition influences the determination of a minimum cost combination. While exports are composed mostly of bulk cargo like sugar and minerals, the import trade consists principally of packaged goods.

Cuba's export business does not need the regularity of transport service which its import freight necessarily demands. Only the export of perishable goods like fruits and fresh vegetables, especially when in season, depends on regular and frequent sailings. Most imported merchandise, on the other hand, needs a stable and reliable service, because that is the only way to enable the importers to accommodate their orders in foreign countries to market conditions at home. The more valuable the articles are and the more stable and regular their price and sales volume, the greater will be the inconvenience of large, but occasional, shipments and accordingly the greater also is the importers' appreciation of a regular and frequent service. The availability of such a service makes it possible to carry lower inventories than would be necessary in the case of irregular and occasional shipments of merchandise for which a given, known, demand exists.[9]

It follows that Cuba's international ocean traffic, apart from other problems rendering minimum-cost operations difficult, has to cope with the difference between the needs of the exporters and importers as to regularity of service and the optimum size of the vessel.

Concerning sugar, we have already shown the costs of a homeward voyage in ballast in comparison with the reduction obtained under certain conditions when the vessel returns with an import cargo. The fact, however, that imports usually require regular and frequent service makes coordination between the export and the import service for maximum efficiency or minimized operating costs extremely difficult. Contributing to this also is the fact that the ports in which sugar is loaded and unloaded vary continuously even within given trading zones. Even if we only examine the most stable sector of sugar exports, the one between Cuba and the United States, or, more narrowly still, between ports of Cuba's north coast and those of the Eastern Seaboard of the United States north of Cape Hatteras, and thus strictly limit all possible variations of ports of origin and ports of destination, it is clear that a perfect coordination of this irregular export service with the

---

9. Because there is permanently an excess of capacity not only in the case under examination, dealing with Cuba's regular maritime import service, but, for that matter, in all shipping activities in general, freight rates tend to establish themselves on the long run on a higher level than they would if it were possible to make full use of available transport facilities. However, when this excess capacity is—even partly—only the result of the user's wish to carry lower inventories than he would need in the case of irregular and occasional service, such over-capacity could not in fairness be called wasteful. It is, after all, one way of avoiding waste of capital through excessive inventories. Therefore, the expression "excess capacity" is not synonymous with idle or useless capacity. It seems most probable that when the users of the service pay freight rates that on the long run finance the shipping operator's over-capacity, they do it after carefully calculating the balance between the costs of higher freight rates and those that they would incur from carrying higher inventories.

regular sailings asked for by the import trade can only happen by chance and never permanently. Normally, arrival time in one of the ports mentioned does not coincide with the time convenient for a regular sailing. This being so, the following alternatives for providing service exist: (*a*) the sugar carrier is prepared to take on the import goods and wait in the respective port for the time of departure according to an established schedule; (*b*) the vessel sails out in ballast, i.e., without the export freight of sugar; or (*c*) she returns in ballast. In any event, to attend to regular import service with vessels used for the export trade—which means crossings of varying duration—necessarily implies an excess of tonnage, in other words permanent excess capacity.

With regard to the carrier's size, requirements of exports and imports again differ. In general the most adequate vessels for Cuba's sugar exports are bigger than those needed to carry imports at the lowest possible cost. This imbalance also creates a problem of excess capacity.

It should be stressed that probably the most important of the reasons for excess capacity is the latter. The former loses importance to the extent that regularity of sailings for the import service is a relative factor, applied with a certain degree of laxity. If the carrier of import goods is being used simultaneously for the export of sugar from Cuba, adherence to a strict sailing schedule is relative; where absolute regularity is required, export cargoes will consist of incomplete loads of sugar, or of goods from other countries, not Cuba, which will be carried to the United States.

Some statistics will show the waste of capacity resulting from the differences in the optimum size of vessels operating exclusively either for exports or imports, but not simultaneously for both. We shall focus our attention on the traffic between Cuba and the United States and there again on the Eastern Seaboard and the Gulf of Mexico, since, as has already been pointed out, this traffic is much more balanced than that between Cuba and other countries and regions.

A loading capacity of about 4000 Spanish long tons is the size most appropriate for ships carrying raw sugar from Cuba to the United States. For the import service, on the other hand, a smaller tonnage is generally preferable. A capacity of 4000 tons, apart from other specifications, corresponds to the normally available quantities of raw sugar in most Cuban ports and to the handling facilities in these as well as in the ports of destination. Besides, this tonnage is the most convenient one for the American refineries, and shipments are therefore seldom larger; on the other hand it does frequently happen that smaller loads, down to 2500 tons, and occasionally even below this figure, are accepted.[10]

By way of contrast, if technical maritime conditions and navigational safety allow it—which is not always the case—the most appropriate type of freight carrier for Cuban imports from United States Atlantic Coast and Gulf ports has a

TABLE 9
Dry Cargo Tonnage Carried by Freighters
Entering the Port of Havana,
1956

Metric tons	Number of ships
Under 500	1303
500–1000	634
1000–1500	236
1500–2000	119
2000–2500	67
2500–3000	44
3000–3500	30
3500–4000	14
4000–4500	15
4500–5000	9
Over 5000	29
Total of arrivals	2500

Source: *El Avisador.*

10. Some Cuban ports at times would have available raw sugar cargoes up to 9000 long tons or even considerably more, and some of the refineries might be able to accept such quantities; but such shipments would mean so much excess capacity of the vessel for purposes of returning with imports that the costs involved preclude such a possibility.

capacity of less than 4000 tons. Table 9 shows the tonnage of dry cargo brought to Havana in 1956 by 2500 ships. The figures are grouped according to the quantities carried by the respective number of freighters.

Table 9 shows that most arrivals were of ships of less than 1500 tons. Obviously the freight frequently consists of merchandise occupying more cubic space than is needed by a ton of sugar. If, however, the cargo consists of rice, soy or wheat flour, potatoes, or any other bagged goods, there is hardly ever a substantial cubic space difference from sugar and probably never one that exceeds 20 per cent.

In conclusion, we repeat that the discrepancy between optimum tonnage of export and import freight carriers results in excess capacity for the import trade whenever the ships are used for both purposes. This operation can therefore not be carried out under minimum cost conditions. The influence of this fact on import freight rates cannot be denied, the more so since it does not seem feasible in the extremely competitive export freight market to shift even part of the cost of the excess capacity to this sector. This is particularly true in periods of depression in the maritime market.

If we turn from the movement of dry cargo between Cuba and the United States to that between Cuba and other parts of the world, we notice an even greater discrepancy between the requirements of the trade and the carrying capacity of the vessels. It is axiomatic in ocean transport economics that the greater the distance, the greater has to be the volume of cargo in order to reduce unit costs by spreading the fixed costs more widely. Even though a Cuban raw sugar carrier may have to call on more than one Cuban port for the completion of eight to ten thousand long tons and thereby may suffer delays that will cause higher costs per vessel and voyage, such increase will easily be outweighed by savings on other accounts. Since the products that can be imported from distant regions to Cuba represent a relatively small tonnage, outgoing traffic from the island to such regions and return trips to it are uneconomical on a sustained basis. This is the reason why such traffic is mostly operated by tramps and, to some extent, by ships that use Cuba only as a port of call on their world-wide routes. Fortunately, Cuba's importance as sugar purveyor for the markets of the world and her excellent geo-economic position attract a sufficient number of ships to attend to the needs of her trade. In addition, the already mentioned mixed cargo-passenger service contributes to fulfill her needs.[11]

Economies of Scale in Cuba's International Maritime Freight Transport

THE OPTIMUM SIZE OF VESSELS

The previous presentation of the principal factors that determine the optimum size of ships in Cuba's international ocean traffic, may be summarized as follows: [12]

For routes of limited export and import traffic, for example,

11. It follows from this that air traffic competition in passenger service will also be detrimental to the transport of cargo. A maritime passenger route was forced out of business by air competition, and this has interrupted and diminished modest but necessary freight services that were also being rendered.

12. This analysis of the optimum size of vessels operating Cuba's international freight transport focuses on the basic point for economies of scale, namely, the proper relation between the size of the vessel and the volume of freight, both in imports and in exports. We shall not refer to the strictly technical reasons, inherent to the size alone of the vessel but independent of the available export and import freight, which explain the possibility of cost advantages through increase in size within certain limits. It is known that while the capacity of a ship grows by the cube of its dimensions, the water resistance increases approximately in proportion to the area in contact with the water, and this area grows proportionally to the square of the dimensions. Consequently, a big ship needs less horsepower per ton for moving at a given speed or attains greater speed than a smaller vessel with the same horsepower per ton. If more speed is not required, there will be an economy in the size of the engine rooms. On the other hand, construction costs per ton tend to decrease with increases in its loading capacity. The same applies to the costs of the crew.

Havana–Miami, a small freighter, or a ship built mainly for passenger service with a limited cargo capacity, is sufficient.

Routes on which refined sugar freight is transported principally and which supply the import trade with about 500 metric tons per voyage, like those, for example, from Havana to the southern Atlantic Seaboard ports of the United States, require vessels that can carry some 1000 to 1500 tons of refined sugar for adequate service.

For routes on which export freight may consist of complete raw sugar cargoes, and imports per voyage of 1000 to 2000 metric tons, vessels of between 2250 and 4000 long tons of raw sugar carrying capacity, will be the most convenient ones.

For the export of sugar to the so-called "world market," i.e., countries other than the United States, tonnage must be superior to the above figures. The unavailability of stable return cargoes encourages the use of tramps of some 10,000 tons to carry exports; for the import trade, tramps of similar size are used when complete cargoes are carried. Mainly, however, this traffic is serviced by regular freight liners calling on Cuban ports, and by mixed vessels, i.e., passenger ships with limited freight capacity.

THE OPTIMUM NUMBER OF VESSELS

An increase in the number of ships servicing a particular route is another way of achieving economies of scale. A shipping concern may find a situation in which, at least potentially, there exists a sufficiently attractive volume of available freight. The concern may then be able to increase its market share through a more intensive service by adding more vessels to its fleet and coordinating their schedules in such a way as to make the greatest possible use of their loading capacity. A hypothetical example based on Cuban traffic will illustrate this.

Let us suppose a route with the following characteristics: exports of raw sugar from ports of Cuba's north coast to Baltimore; return freight of general merchandise from Baltimore consigned to Havana. As has been pointed out, raw sugar exports imply irregular sailings from Cuba, while imports, particularly those of general merchandise, require at least a minimum of regularity.

The average round trip will take about twenty-one days: three days for the stowage of raw sugar in the north Cuban port; five days for sailing to Baltimore; three days of unloading and one of loading there; five days of sailing to Havana; two days of unloading there; and, finally, one to two days for sailing in ballast to whatever port in which the next sugar cargo is taken on.

In view of the convenience of regular sailings from Baltimore to Havana, a monthly service with fixed days of departure might be considered. Since for the round trip an average of about twenty-one days is needed, the ship would obviously lose about nine days per month waiting in port for its sailing day. If regular sailings from Baltimore were increased to two per month, one on the first and one on the fifteenth, these naturally could not be served by a single ship. Two would be needed and each of them would also lose about nine days each month. If, however, a weekly service from Baltimore to Havana were to be established, i.e., departures on the first, eighth, fifteenth, twenty-second, and twenty-ninth, such service could be effected by three vessels in this way: ship A sails on the first, ship B on the eighth, ship C on the fifteenth, ship A on the twenty-second, and ship B on the twenty-ninth. In the next month ship C would have the first and ship B the last departure. And in the third month the schedule of the first month would be repeated.

All in all, the three ships would lose perhaps one or two days a month and the service would have been increased fivefold through only a threefold increase in the number of vessels. Or, if the number of ships was raised by 50 per cent—from two to three—the service could be increased by 150 per cent. In view of the characteristics of the route and supposing that the available cargo volume justifies a weekly service, it is easy to see that three would be the optimum number of ships for this service.

Theoretically, an operator would be able to supply this service with only two vessels owned by him or held under long-term charters, and a third one chartered per voyage when needed. Then his ships A and B would leave Baltimore the first month according to the following itinerary: on the first, A; on the eighth, B; on the twenty-second, A; and on the twenty-ninth, B. In the second month A could only sail on the fifteenth and B on the twenty-second. The third month's sailing dates for A would be the eighth and twenty-ninth, while B could sail only on the fifteenth. For all other voyages, those not performed by these two ships, i.e., the fifteenth of the first month, the eighth and twenty-ninth of the second month, etc., a vessel would have to be chartered for one voyage only, either the crossing Baltimore–Havana (trip down), or the round trip carrying Cuban sugar back to Baltimore. In actual fact, however, such a possibility is remote and could happen only occasionally, because it would hardly be feasible to obtain an appropriate carrier for just the right dates, and failure to do so would jeopardize the regularity of the service. A charter contract for one voyage only, therefore, will be a last recourse used by a line with strict regular sailing schedules in the case of an accident which prevents the sailing of the regular liner. Only in such an emergency is it customary to charter a substitute vessel for just one, or—if necessary—several, consecutive trips.

THE NUMBER AND COMBINATION OF ROUTES
AND UTILIZATION OF THE VESSELS

Economies of scale can be achieved by a maritime enterprise not only through increase in the number and capacity of its fleet, but also through better utilization of the vessels, if the number of routes can be increased and coordinated.

Let us return once more to the hypothetical case of the route between Cuban north-coast ports and Baltimore, with a return trip from Baltimore to Havana, from where the ship again proceeds to another Cuban port. The inadvisability of establishing fortnightly departures on this route has already been pointed out. The most practical solution has also been shown: to increase the service from two monthly sailings, one every second week, to weekly departures, using three instead of two boats. Apart from everything else, this is naturally feasible only when the available payload is sufficient. Should the potential freight, however, not suffice for the route in question or, to be more concrete, for the Baltimore–Havana run, what other alternative might exist if the shipping line is also operating on other routes or could start such operations?

The simplest case would be the hypothesis that such a line operates a fortnightly direct service from Baltimore to Mexican or Venezuelan ports. In this case Havana could be included as an additional port of call. The convenience of doing so would naturally depend on a series of circumstances, of which the following deserve mention: the vessel's speed, because time lost with entering and remaining in the port of Havana must be made up through speedier voyages; a new arrangement of the ports of call, which may mean time lost through not loading or unloading over weekends, or increases of costs by doing just that; the distance between consecutive ports, which must be great enough to recover, at least in part, the time lost in Havana; and, lastly, the excess capacity of the vessel or vessels, which must warrant the inclusion of the port of Havana in the voyage.

To sum up, under these circumstances and a number of others that must be taken into consideration in each individual case, a shipping concern may make its fleet operate more profitably by adding to its routes or extending existing ones, thus extending its traffic network.

THE AVAILABILITY OF VESSELS:
THE CHARTER BUSINESS

In addition to the factors already mentioned, there is one of special importance for an understanding of economies of scale inherent in the structure of Cuban shipping concerns. It is the chartering of vessels from other owners.

A shipping firm can, as has been pointed out, operate either with boats of its own or with ships that are chartered for varying periods of time. The use of self-owned ships usually implies incurring costs to be classified as "fixed" for a much longer period than would be the case in operating chartered vessels. The capital costs of the latter tend to be variable.

Both ways of operation have their advantages and disadvantages in the short and in the long run. Their impact and influence depend on each company's circumstances and the scope and area of its operations. As a first approximation, however, it appears that for solid and solvent concerns with ample financial resources, operation with vessels of their own offers definite long-term advantages. Weaker firms, on the other hand, with a less stable position in the market and limited resources, may do better with chartered freighters, especially over the most relevant time horizon, that is to say, the short and medium term. Operating a self-owned fleet would not give them the same advantages. But even this statement is not always valid and it happens frequently that small maritime concerns start operations with their own ships. Which alternative is preferable may also depend on the instability of traffic in general or on particular routes and on the kind and composition of outward- and homeward-bound freight.

For an analysis of this problem it may help to imagine the case of a firm with limited resources which decides to go into the shipping business. Its first aim for profit maximization will be to get a firm foothold in the market and for this it will obviously need a minimum number of ships. The efficient way of obtaining them will as a rule consist of charter contracts for certain periods of time. It is very possible that this imaginary firm may employ a staff of efficient and capable managers and administrators and that it can count on a potential clientele and consequently on a volume of cargo, foreseeable with relative certainty. Not having, however, enough financial resources for the purchase of adequate vessels, it may decide to use time-charter ships for its activities. According to the demand for the service and the possibilities of the organization, additional charter contracts for convenient periods of time may be made, and thus the firm may grow and benefit from some economies of scale.

The consolidation of the firm's position in the market will sooner or later, according to circumstances, create the desire for and possibility of acquiring its own vessels. The degree of this incentive will be determined by the desire to maximize profits, given, on the one hand, the rate of growth of the business and, on the other, the greater risks that are normally inherent in operating self-owned vessels.

This, however, is not always the procedure in starting a maritime business. There do exist cases of firms starting in a small way, but with a fleet of their own. There are, of course, reasons which explain this. These new entrepreneurs may be men who have gathered experience in shipping as owners of a fleet of schooners or operators of a modest dockyard, or even as captains or officers in the employ of other shipping firms. Through any of these possibilities or through a combination of several, they may have gained experience and perhaps even (as Marshall would say) through a stroke of luck—not unusual in wartime—may have obtained not only knowledge and connections inside the maritime business, but also a certain capital. The latter may finance the purchase of at least one ship, usually small and already depreciated, at a bargain price, with which they may be able to sail and offer the kind of service regarded as unattractive by more powerful enterprises on account of low freight rates. With only a minimum organization, they keep away from routes where earnings are high, routes which are therefore already in the hands of stronger firms, avoid ports where costs are high, and do not attempt to handle volumes of cargo requiring regular sailings and modern efficient equipment; thus they will either prosper, hold their own, and finally compete with the old established firms, or languish and in the end disappear.

Proof of the possibility of success of a new maritime business operating with its own vessels right from the start lies in the frequency of their registration in Cuba's maritime traffic lists.[13] The basic reason for this fact lies in the relatively low price of the ships which reduces the risk of operating them.

The real world is infinitely complex and it may well happen that in some circumstances a small firm decides to enter the business by using chartered vessels, while at other times similar firms may decide that it is preferable to own their ships. At any rate, it is a matter of record that very often, when a small shipping concern decides to expand, it does so by adding chartered ships to its fleet. In attempting to pinpoint the motivation for this, it must be stressed that what is characteristic and essential in a maritime business does not pertain to the vessel, or vessels, but rather lies in the general organization of the firm and, in particular, the potential volume of available cargo to be carried between certain ports at a given freight rate. This is the true basis of any possibility for success. Anybody able to obtain freight and to organize a going concern can become a shipper; vessels are of relatively minor importance because there are so many ways of acquiring them. What counts is specialization in the production of the service and the capacity to meet the risks it entails.

It is important to stress this point precisely because of the existence of some solid Cuban shipping firms which operate a number of ships well in excess of what their financial resources

13. These small shippers tend to service routes which, in order to be profitable, require cheap and old boats which are not found easily in the time-charter market. This is another important reason for operating with ships of their own.

would permit them to own. But their management is capable
and they possess fine connections among the users of the service. Their expansion is due, therefore, to a maximum utilization
of the personal qualities of their directors, taking advantage of
their organizational, administrative, and executive capacity,
and overcoming lack of capital through time-charter contracts,
thus adding to their fleet the number of vessels needed for
expansion.

TABLE 10
Time-Charter Rates and Freight Rates
in Principal Traffic Routes
(dollars per ton)

	1957		1958
	January	December	February
General index (base 1951)	83	43	39.8
Time-charter			
Liberties (10–12 months)	$ 6.15	$ 2.15	$1.80
Coal			
Hampton Roads–Rio	14.00	4.75	4.55
Hampton Roads–W. Italy	14.00	4.25	4.00
Hampton Roads–Japan	22.00	9.25	6.75
Grain			
U.S. Gulf ports–Rotterdam	17.25	4.75	4.00
North Pacific–Japan	15.00	5.75	5.50
Sugar			
Cuba–U.S.A., north of Hatteras	.54	.34	.33
Cuba–U.S. Gulf ports	.45	.32	.30
Cuba–Japan	27.50	10.78	8.40

Source: Maritime Research Inc., *Chartering Annual, 1957;* Shipowners
Agency, *Weekly Market Report,* Feb. 21 and March 1, 1958; American
and Overseas Shipbrokerage Inc., *Weekly Market Letter,* Feb. 21, 1958;
New York Times, March 3, 1958.

We have shown that medium-sized concerns are making use
of the indisputable advantages of chartering to increase their
share of the market and that this is their way of eliminating,
or considerably reducing, the burden of fixed costs which own-

ership of the fleet implies. Not only financial limitations [14] can thus be overcome, but also—at the sacrifice of possible greater profits—the risk of losses. And the latter is at least as important for a medium-sized business as the chance of greater profits; how serious such risks can be in this activity, with its constant and often violent ups and downs due to cyclical fluctuations of world trade, is well known.[15] Table 10 is based on various sources and illustrates these fluctuations in the recent past. This table shows the enormous slump in freight rates for some commodities of which great volumes are transported in world trade. A shipping firm operating with its own vessels in these markets obviously found itself at the end of 1957 in a situation vastly different from what it was when the year began. At that time earnings not only covered all costs, but also made operations extremely profitable; by December not only had all profits disappeared, but income from operations would have no longer been sufficient for amortization and—where relevant—financing, unless the vessel had been acquired in a period of extreme depression and therefore at a very low price.

What would have been the comparable position of a firm operating with chartered boats? We may take as representative the charter rates of ships of the "Liberty" type, since these in the postwar years acted as pace-setters for the whole market. Although depending on when vessels were chartered, on the conditions and duration of the charter contract, and, of course, on market expectations, in general the available carrying capacity accommodated itself amazingly well to users' demand, and operating costs also adapted themselves to a high degree to existing freight rates.

How expectations about future market behavior interplay with the time at which the ship is obtained, whether by charter

14. Occasionally a growing concern has even found it necessary to sell some of its own ships, thus freeing liquid funds to meet, partially or totally, its growing obligations.

15. Frank Cyril James, *Cyclical Fluctuations in the Shipping and Shipbuilding Industries* (Philadelphia: University of Pennsylvania Press, 1927).

or by purchase, and with the time for which the vessel is available can be shown by the following example: Suppose that of two very similar shipping operators one, A, decided in January, 1957, to buy a vessel identical in the main characteristics (age, carrying capacity, speed, etc.) to one that the other, B, was chartering at the same time. The purchase price was high.[16] Suppose further that both operators had at the time sufficient capital for the purchase of one of the ships. Since A acquired one, while B preferred to charter one, it seems evident that their forecasts were different; the first must have been optimistic about future freight market developments, the other pessimistic. The decline that occurred in 1957 proved the pessimist right and his success was the greater the more charter price and charter period adapted themselves to the freight rate curve.

Now let us consider the hypothetical situation of the two operators in January, 1958. This time the assumption is that the ideas of both men about the future of the maritime market are identical and correct, both being convinced that the market decline has reached its low point and that in the near future a long period of recovery will begin. In this situation, leaving out the many other considerations that would have to be taken into account in an actual case, the advisable thing in January, 1958, would have been the acquisition, not the charter, of the vessel, provided, of course, that the shippers and the sellers of the ships make sufficiently different forecasts. Actually, however, since shipper A had purchased a vessel in January, 1957, and had suffered the unfortunate setback caused by the sudden, unforeseen market decline, he might not be in a position to afford a new purchase. In contrast, B, with his financial

16. "Liberty" ships at the beginning of 1957 were priced at about £600,000 or more; at the beginning of 1958 the quotation had slumped to about £200,000 and at the middle of that year it fluctuated around £130,000. The price depended partly on the possibility of free transfer of the boat according to the buyer's and seller's national flags and partly on the ship's state of repair.

resources at least intact, could easily exchange the boat he chartered in 1957 for one of his own. His position would definitely be much better than that of A.

It goes without saying that in the reverse case, i.e., if the freight market had shown an upward trend and maintained it for a longer period, the optimist, A, would have been the lucky one and reaped a better harvest than B, who did not speculate on a rise.

We repeat that reality is very complex. Still, there is no doubt that for an enterprise with limited resources the risks involved in operating with chartered vessels are considerably less than those of ownership of the fleet. Accepting further the advisability of slow but solid growth for any firm, instead of a meteoric but precarious rise, it can be said that the Cuban shipping firms' practice of chartering their vessels is logical and praiseworthy. The main asset of these firms, at least the solid ones, lies in their managerial and administrative capacities. Making the best possible use of these, they prefer to expand by means of time-charter contracts rather than with self-owned boats. This admittedly sometimes forces them to sacrifice the highest possible profits, but it also reduces their risks and assures them of staying in business.

Another advantage inherent in the time-charter business of Cuba's ocean traffic with the United States—the only really interesting one—results from the lack of stable cargo volume. Stability varies, of course, on the different routes and has cyclical and seasonal dimensions. Exports of sugar are not subject to severe fluctuations, while, on the other hand, imports suffer ups and downs, depending strongly on Cuba's national income and—in some cases, such as rice and potatoes—on its domestic production. But even sugar exports move in cycles during the year. In some months they reach their maximum, only to decline in others, mainly towards the end of the year. Adjustment to these variations of freight volume by employing time charter is under all circumstances advisable. Thus the waste of tonnage which would result from ownership of the carriers is avoided.

Finally, there is one further characteristic of Cuba's international ocean freight market which, together with the instability of the volume of cargo, enhances the convenience of operating with chartered vessels. Freight rates for the principal export commodities, especially for sugar, are subject to extreme fluctuations. When sugar freight rates are so low that they do not cover the costs of the service, it is naturally most useful to be able to cancel sailings or replace bigger carriers with smaller ones. Thus at least the import service can continue to operate with boats of the most appropriate number and size for the requirements of this traffic.

The Management, Administration, and Size of Shipping Firms

The larger an enterprise, the more can management function through coordinated decentralized departments with individual specializations. In a small shipping firm the main tasks involved in supplying the service—that is to say, making ships available—and the duties related to cost supervision, insurance, and forecasting, as well as sales promotion (soliciting cargoes), inevitably fall on a very small number of people, who tend to be part of the management. These may well be individuals of sound judgment, with ample experience and with that special instinct that characterizes the successful businessman. But, absorbed by the multiplicity of problems that require their attention, it is quite probable that they will not be able to use their expertise with the care and accuracy required by the rapidly shifting circumstances of an expanding business. When such an expansion occurs, it is therefore advisable to strengthen the organization by bringing in specialized personnel who will be able to take over a number of tasks; the previously concentrated responsibility will inevitably have to be subdivided. The former managers at the same time should retain an overall guiding and supervising position.

Thus it will be possible to create a functional managerial and administrative structure which, once its specialized services or departments are established, will yield increasing economies as the enterprise grows, since the departments will not have to grow in the same proportion.

One need only compare two enterprises of different size, both engaged in Cuba's international maritime cargo traffic. The smaller one would inflate its costs excessively were it to divide its promotional activities between two separate departments: one to solicit export cargoes and one for imports. One person, or at least a few people, will have to handle both jobs and some others as well. In any event, the firm that is used to a modest volume of traffic will neither attempt nor need to create a more complex organization, since for the import trade it can largely rely on the services of agents abroad. The larger firm, on the other hand, will have at its service an export department—say, to solicit sugar shipments—and a body of salesmen who will solicit import cargoes in Cuba. It may even have its offices in some important foreign ports, and these subsidiaries may in turn be linked with agencies in other, smaller, ports. Another difference is that the smaller firm probably does not have a staff that specializes exclusively in the chartering business; it therefore cannot follow the fluctuations of the market so closely that it is able at any given moment to decide what special opportunities it offers. This, and the previously noted points, may largely explain why smaller shipowners seem to prefer to operate their own, cheaply acquired, vessels. By way of contrast, the larger firms, working through a specialized department, will follow the time-charter market quotations closely, will have available the information and offers of the brokers and thus will be able to judge the overall situation on the basis of pertinent data.

Once a wide network has been organized to supply the service efficiently and to obtain shipments, economies of scale will emerge from the mere growth of the volume transported. Costs will not rise significantly in the sugar export department when —within certain limits—its shipments rise, nor will the time charter department's costs rise when the number of vessels so contracted increases.

All managerial activity in a shipping enterprise, inasmuch as it is market oriented, operates at three levels. Each of these has its own problems which are made more complex by their mutual interactions and connections. They are competition among shipping firms, competition among goods to be shipped (both the existing and the ever-present potential competition), and changes in the direction of trade. Competition with rivals requires as much freedom to maneuver, or more, when it is "oligopolistic" as when it involves a large number of firms. The "conference" system—including that applicable to Cuba's trade—continuously tests the ability of each enterprise to match its own interests with those of the other group members.[17]

Concerning competition among commodities to be transported, shippers cannot prevent a continuous process of substitution of goods, including the disappearance of traditional products and the appearance of new ones. Nor can they avoid the fact that exporters and importers with whom they have had close business ties may decline and disappear or be replaced by others with whom contacts will have to be established anew.

Changes in the destination of traffic are the result of many causes, including the two types of competition discussed above. We have seen to what degree the success of a maritime

17. Competition with rivals exists not only among the shipping firms themselves but also with other means of transportation. Since Cuba is an island, international freight traffic would seem to be free from competition by the railroads; in reality, however, the railroad ferries provide such competition.

enterprise depends on good management and administration. A growing volume of operations in turn is the best way of making full use of its managerial and administrative capacities. The size and growth potential of a firm, however, do not only depend on its internal economies, but also on the inter-firm relations and interconnections existing in the industry. In other words, the position of one firm vis-à-vis the rest and the over-all size of the industry are other pertinent determinants of a firm's growth. We are inclined to feel that in Cuba's international cargo traffic there are firms with the necessary managerial ability. On the other hand, however, precisely the structural characteristics of this traffic [18] lead us to conclude that the size of the principal concerns has nearly reached the limits imposed by the structure of the industry; therefore, we venture to assert that the capacity of certain shipping enterprises neither has been nor can in the future be made full use of. In other words, certain Cuban shipping operators have only been able to subsist and prosper because of their ability, but it is quite possible—although such a speculation is completely academic—that they might have derived much more profit from their intelligence and dynamism in other activities, which would have given more scope to the full development of their talents.

The Costs of Sales Promotion
in the Cuban Maritime Business

In our consideration of operating costs we mentioned the so-called costs of sales, which are characteristic of many im-

18. The market is very competitive in the export sector; in the import traffic the most important firms are also attempting to maintain their market shares, as is witnessed by the conference system. In such a market the price for the transfer of customers from one firm to another is very high. (See E. A. G. Robinson, *The Structure of Competitive Industry*, p. 82.) This is why on some rare occasions the purchase of one concern by another has been used as a means of expansion.

perfect markets, and we argued that such costs are not important in freight traffic. As already noted, the structure of Cuba's maritime cargo routes and markets also makes this proposition applicable to this case. A breakdown by exports and imports according to commodity components will confirm this statement.

By far the most important part of the export trade is not serviced by regular liners and consists of complete bulk cargoes of sugar. Sugar freight rates are formed in a market that is subject to considerable price competition and in which it is therefore impossible to obtain monopolistic positions or advantages through advertising and publicity. A certain minimum of soliciting is obviously needed to give information to exporters about sailing dates and particular conditions and characteristics of vessels. This, however, is the work assigned to a very small staff and its costs are negligible in proportion to the value of any given contract.

Nor is intense solicitation necessary for other exports carried by regular lines, because users know about usual sailing dates and the existence of the service. Lack of competition, caused by specialization of the service, for example, refrigeration for the export of fresh fruits and vegetables, likewise makes intense advertising superfluous.

In the importation of bulk shipments or complete cargoes of raw materials the situation is similar to that of sugar exports; promotional costs tend to be practically nonexistent, especially when, as in some cases in the Cuban ocean traffic, the importing firm itself is the owner of the vessels carrying the freight. This frequently happens in the liquid fuel trade, which represents a high percentage of total imports.

For the import of other products from abroad, the costs of sales promotion are also negligible, because of supply and demand conditions of the market. On the supply side, these costs decrease strongly when, as happens frequently, the number of competitors on a given route is small, or when they belong to a pool in which sailing schedules are regulated and also cargoes are distributed according to mutual agreements. This occurs in the case of substantial freight volumes arriving in Cuban ports from some American ports on the Gulf of Mexico. On the demand side, a small number of importers frequently handle import commodities with the help of shipping concerns with whom long association has established strong ties of friendship and habit. No sales promotion is therefore necessary. Even though there are some types of cargo imported by a greater number of small and medium-sized importers for which the shipper usually obtains more profitable freight rates, and for which his efforts of solicitation in this sector must therefore be more perseverant, the costs of such work are also negligible in comparison to the income derived from gross freights.

On the whole, as already noted, overall sales costs in the Cuban maritime cargo service probably do not reach 1 per cent of the total costs, or the total gross income derived from freights.

Freight Rates and Transport Costs by Type of Merchandise

After having briefly outlined the general behavior and determinants of the costs of Cuba's international maritime traffic, and the insignificance of the so-called sales costs in spite of imperfect market conditions, we may examine a few examples to see to what extent and in which items freight rates are related to the cost of production of the service.

For exports, a breakdown has already been made of the components of the cost of transporting sugar from a north Cuban port (Nuevitas) to an American northeast-coast port (Baltimore). By adapting these data to the differences in distance, and therefore duration, of the voyage, fuel consumption, etc., we can obtain a good idea of the relation between costs and freight rates for the transport of sugar from a port on Cuba's north coast to one on the southeastern seaboard of the United States or the Gulf of Mexico. In Chapter 2 the close correspondence between costs and freight rates for the transport of raw sugar to any part of the coast of the United States was already noted. Similarly, freight rate variations between shipments of sugar from Cuba's south and north coast basically reflect differences in the production cost of the service. In a strongly competitive market this cannot be otherwise.

It would undoubtedly be interesting to analyze the cost composition of ocean transportation of other exports for a better understanding of their interconnection with freight rates. Such an analysis would be even more interesting for types of merchandise that require special handling, like fruits and vegetables with their need for refrigeration. But, in view of the small proportion which this trade represents in Cuba's total exports, the space required for such an analysis would be exorbitant.

Instead, we will focus our attention on the relation between costs and freight rates of some important staple dry cargoes imported from the United States, since these, as already noted, are of particular interest. Such a study, however, is not easy, because a cost calculation for the transportation of each kind of merchandise is so difficult that it has been said that "in the transport business the general opinion prevails that the cost, and therefore the profits, of moving any particular product cannot be determined." [19]

In effect, total revenues and total costs are frequently used to determine profits or losses during a given accounting period. The management of a well-directed firm will of course discover the failure of a particular cargo to produce profits. Experience and even intuition will guide the businessman in this respect; but it is undoubtedly true that occasionally long pe-

19. See Henry B. Cooley, *Freight Transportation for Profit* (Cambridge, Md.: Cornell Maritime Press, 1946), p. 34.

riods of time can pass in which this fails to happen. Sometimes, however, that which is believed detrimental and unprofitable [20] is in reality the opposite.

The basic difficulty in establishing a direct relationship between costs and the freight rates charged by the shipping enterprise for the transport of a given merchandise lies in the previously noted fact that such an enterprise has to be regarded as a producer of multiple services. The allocation of cost items to each of the services rendered is an extremely complicated task.

For accounting purposes the correct distribution of the items should be based on a well-founded economic judgment, derived mainly from the characteristics of the firm—the volume and kinds of goods transported, the organization and equipment used, the routes to be covered, etc.—and, in particular, its own established position in the market in general. In fact, a proper distribution of the cost items depends on innumerable factors and circumstances which are subject in varying degrees to constant and often abrupt changes. Any such calculation will therefore always be at least somewhat arbitrary. Nevertheless, a close examination of the most relevant factors will at least show why the calculation is arbitrary, even if it cannot be reduced to reasonable terms. There will always remain a substantial margin of doubt, which in practice can only be surmounted by decisions from the men in charge of policy about the prices and the kinds of transport services to be supplied. The possibility of error, however, is of such magnitude that it amply explains the enormous risks inherent in the maritime business. It also explains the absolute necessity for such an enterprise to be guided by a management that is able to face and reduce these risks methodically, linking the

20. Differentiating between successive periods of time, it has already been pointed out that what matters is often not the highest monetary profit, but that occasionally an immediate loss may be the prerequisite for later gains.

interests of their own firm to those of the users as well as of competitors by methods already referred to.

Table 11 shows the freight rates and cost structures of three examples of products shipped from the United States to the port of Havana. Except for those cost items which, as will be explained, are automatically connected with the respective product or group of goods, the rest has been allocated mainly according to personal judgments. The result thus obtained will help to establish the basic principles that have to be applied in the setting of freight rates for the different kinds of merchandise—the particular costs inherent in their transport as well as the possibilities open to shipping enterprises for a maximum utilization of their capacity. As such enterprises are, within certain limits, characterized by decreasing costs, they can and must establish a discriminatory pricing policy with this object in mind.

The construction of the table is an attempt to find a starting point for tracing the basic structure of freight rates and to inquire into their interrelations with costs. This in turn will, at least indirectly, explain the calculation of profits derived from Cuba's international ocean transport operations.

The components of Table 11 are (*a*) freight rates for a group of commodities for which they are particularly high; (*b*) freight rates for the transport of potatoes; (*c*) freight rates for soy beans. Freight rates for "miscellaneous products" represent an average of rates charged for some of the goods transported on certain routes. Some of their distinctive features are that the special care required for their handling, their cubic space, and the regularity of the demand for them are all superior to those of potatoes and soy beans.

The stowage, unloading, and pier-fee items are either derived from existing specific rates or are estimated on the basis of experience. Their computation and application to each product, therefore, does not offer unsurmountable difficulties, although the available figures are debatable. Agency commissions in the United States are, in practice, uniform and therefore only give rise to doubts when the agency office belongs to the shipping enterprise itself. Really serious problems, however, arise with the allocation of the other cost items to each type of merchandise.

TABLE 11

Estimated Freight Rates and Distribution of Transport Costs for Certain Products from United States Ports to Havana in 1956

	Miscellaneous products		Potatoes		Soy beans	
Freight per ton	$64.00	100%	$25.00	100%	$13.00	100%
Costs per ton:						
Pier charges, U.S.A.	7.94	12.40	3.50	14.00	*	*
Stowage, U.S.A.	7.23	11.30	3.00	12.00	3.04	23.38
Unloading, Havana	2.50	3.91	2.00	8.00	1.50	11.54
Pier charges, Havana	13.00	20.31	4.00	16.00	4.00	30.77
Agency costs, U.S.A.	5.60	8.75	2.18	8.75	1.13	8.75
Overtime & lost time	2.08	3.25	.82	3.25	.42	3.25
Claims	.69	1.08	.27	1.08	.14	1.08
Vessels & fuel	16.00	25.00	6.25	25.00	3.25	25.00
Port fees, U.S.A.	1.28	2.00	.50	2.00	.26	2.00
Port fees, Havana	.64	1.00	.25	1.00	.13	1.00
Sundry	3.20	5.00	1.25	5.00	.65	5.00
Total	$60.16	95.00%	$24.02	96.08%	$14.52	111.77%
Profit or (loss)	$ 3.84	5.00%	$ .98	3.92%	($1.25)	(11.77%)

* Negligible.

Note: See pages 101–2 for computations of figures.

Concerning stowage, unloading, and pier charges, a detailed breakdown would be necessary to understand the differences in each particular case. For the purpose of our present study, however, such details will not be needed. It will be sufficient to point to a few of a long list of reasons for these differences: the weight and compactness of the product, which may reduce or increase the difficulties of handling from pier to hold or from hold to terminal exit; the necessity of stowing the goods so as to avoid shifts in the course of the voyage, which might damage them or the hull of the ship; dangers involved in the handling (explosives); congestions on the pier; space and conditions of warehousing; the attitudes and habits of labor, etc.[21]

Reference must be made to a point that will receive further attention in the following chapter: the different meanings of the concept of maritime freight rates. In the computation of the cost elements of such freights, strictly speaking, one should omit the items of stowage, unloading, and pier charges. In a wider sense, on the other hand, they ought to be included and still others should be added. The freight rates of Table 11 are in effect those that are usually charged by the shipping firm for reasons of convenience to the users. Pier fees for soy beans in the various United States ports have not been included because their negligible cost is paid for only partly by the shipper, while the rest is directly charged to the importer by the forwarder, together with other costs. In reality, therefore, freights in the wider sense are somewhat higher than those shown as paid to the shipping operator in the traffic between Cuba and the United States. But ocean freight rates in the strict sense of the word, or those that directly interest the operator, are obtained by subtracting handling costs on piers and terminals from the items of the table. The remaining cost components will now be mentioned.

The estimation of these costs, which are the vital ingredients of the maritime enterprise, is based on empirical data derived from annual statements which embody the results of moving a variety of goods over different routes; this movement has been carried out by equipment, i.e., vessels, of dissimilar characteristics. The results are therefore only an approximation to our goal of examining the relationship between the transport costs of any given merchandise and its respective freight rates.

The most important costs are those connected with the ship and with fuel. The costs of the ship have been calculated on the assumption that the carriers are chartered, because this,

21. For an excellent treatise on these points, see Charles L. Sauerbier, *Maritime Cargo Operations* (New York: John Wiley & Sons, 1956).

as has been explained, is the system most appropriate for Cuba's international ocean traffic. Items that are only relevant to self-owned vessels have not been shown separately; such items include the crew's payroll and the provisioning, maintenance, and insurance of the ship. These have been allocated in a fixed proportion to the different freights charged for the transport of the goods used as examples. Although such an allocation is arbitrary, it is precisely this arbitrariness which shows the principles that have to be applied for the setting of each particular freight rate. A cost distribution of this kind evidently results in a considerable loss for the transport of soy beans, while potatoes show modest profits and "miscellaneous products" larger ones. In fact, however, neither does the transport of soy beans *necessarily* produce a loss, nor is it certain that the apparent profits shown in the other two cases really exist.

To understand this, we must examine the several cases that can actually occur and to apply some time-honored elementary economic theory. To prove that it is the transport of soy beans which produces losses, one must assume that on the route on which this product is being transported no other merchandise of sufficient volume and commanding higher freights is available. In such a case the transport could obviously not be made at prevailing freight rates, except by an improbably cheap vessel. If, however, other kinds of cargo can be transported on the route in sufficient quantities at better rates, the shipping of soy beans can and must be considered as an additional producer of marginal, or additional, revenue. From this income only marginal expenses or costs, derived directly from the handling of the additional cargo, will have to be subtracted. In case these marginal costs do not exceed revenues derived from such cargo (soy beans), no loss will result from its transport.

The marginalist criterion will also have to be applied when, as is frequently the case, a shipping enterprise operates on several routes and on one route transports mainly so-called "miscellaneous products," and on another only, or primarily, the soy beans referred to. Even if operations on a whole route yield clear losses, it may still be advantageous to service such a route, provided that no overall loss results to the firm. This would naturally be feasible only in the limited case of operations in imperfect markets and under particular market conditions which would make an especially aggressive freight rate policy advisable. Under such conditions the service might be provided at a loss to avoid the following situations. If the firm failed to offer it, users' demand might raise freight rates to a level which would attract competitors who would take over the available volume of freight in order to strengthen their position and become permanent potential rivals of the old established firms.

Obviously the fact that a particular cargo has to be transported at a freight rate basically governed by marginal costs, not leaving room for allocation of even part of the fixed costs, requires the existence of goods transported at high rates, to which all long-term fixed costs as well as some specific variable ones can be allocated, including in some cases even part of those variable costs that have been incurred through the carrying of products at very low freight rates. If, for example, in our table we transferred all vessel and fuel costs from soy beans to "miscellaneous products," under the given assumptions about the transport of both kinds of goods, losses on the former item would be more than eliminated and profits on the latter reduced.

It is quite clear, therefore, that in his policy decisions about freight rates for any given merchandise, the shipping operator must be guided by cost considerations as well as by the characteristics of the market for each of them. The degree to which different types of merchandise can support higher or lower freight rates depends on the price and income elasticity of the demand for them and on the degree of competition prevailing on the demand as well as on the supply side. If a firm transports several types of merchandise over several routes, it becomes the prototype of a multiple-product firm and decisions about freight rates for the transport of any particular product must conform to this pattern. In the analysis of real data it is always difficult to find really persuasive ways in which to allocate costs to particular products. It is therefore equally difficult to establish irrefutable relations between these costs and the respective freight rates. "Rules of thumb" will always have to be employed in this matter, but an objective study—more elaborate than the present summary one—will yield an answer which, although imperfect, will satisfy these canons of economic analysis.

If it seems unfair to allocate costs in a manner by which some weigh more than proportionally on the freight rates of certain products, it may be well to point out that several authors who have analyzed this aspect of discriminatory pricing policies have come to the same conclusion. It is that as long as the monopoly power of operators is not excessive, the solution outlined above is not only administratively the simplest, but also the most equitable. For Daniel Marx, Jr.[22] price discrimination provides socially satisfactory solutions in decreasing cost industries. He adds that the greatest weakness of price discrimination is that it may be excessive; this indeed has occurred in ocean transportation. But although a certain degree of monopoly power is necessary to be able to discriminate, the existence of actual or potential competition has usually prevented flagrant abuses of such power. In Cuba's international ocean traffic there is not the slightest chance for discriminatory rates on the most important export item, namely, raw sugar. Although for other exports shipped on regular liners a wide range of rates exists, it seems certain that the revenues derived from such cargoes barely cover costs so that offsetting action must be taken for the return freights. As for imports,

22. *International Shipping Cartels*, p. 310.

their heterogeneous composition, the regularity and frequency of the service, and, in short, the imperfectly competitive character of the shipping market, permit a wider range of discriminatory rates. But with the exception of some cases in which losses on export freights are offset, the highest freight rates are usually charged for imports of high unit costs, which also are more frequently luxury items. Food and raw materials, on the other hand, usually pay freight rates that are either competitive or rank low on the general rate scale. Import freight rates can therefore be compared in a way to a combination of import duties and subsidies, made to operate correctly according to economic welfare criteria. This parallel, however, should not be interpreted as a firm assertion until it is borne out by a full inquiry.

4

CUBA'S BALANCE OF INTERNATIONAL PAYMENTS AND NATIONAL INCOME IN RELATION TO THE OCEAN FREIGHT TRAFFIC

WE HAVE STUDIED the main import and export traffic flows and the market structure within which freight rates are formed, as well as the main features of the cost of the service and of the firms that render it. We will now attempt to estimate the significance of ocean freights in Cuba's balance of payments and national income.

Limitations in the availability of statistics prevent a fully satisfactory calculation. But even without being able to achieve the desired quantitative precision, we believe that our estimates are not without qualitative interest. They permit not only an overall view but also an outline of the main details of the picture. When fitted into the right conceptual and factual framework, they may dispel a number of prevailing errors and inaccuracies about the true impact of this item on the balance of payments and the national income.

The Balance of Payments, Cuba's Ocean Traffic, and the Methods of the International Monetary Fund

In the International Monetary Fund's *Balance of Payments Manual* [1] the rules are given for computing the various items

1. International Monetary Fund, *Balance of Payments Manual* (2nd ed.; Washington, D.C., 1950).

contained in this important component of the national accounts. Table V of the *Manual* refers to transportation; the first part concerns income received from abroad, and the second part, payments made abroad. Under "transportation" both that of persons (passengers) and that of goods (freight) are included, as are a number of sub-items connected with the rendering of these services. The means of transport utilized—ship, airplane, railroad, highway—is specified under each of the two main traffic categories.

In this study only the receipts and expenditures for ocean freight transport will be estimated, while the transportation of passengers and that of freight by other means, will be excluded.

Since ocean freight traffic is to be our only concern, it will be useful to begin by clarifying the vitally important concept of the nationality of operators. *Cuban shipping concerns* are those whose center of interest or residence is Cuba, whether the ships that they operate are their own or are chartered and whether these vessels are registered in Cuba or abroad. *Foreign shipping operators,* consequently, are those whose residence or center of interest is not in Cuba, whatever the ownership or place of registration of their vessels.

The Fund's focal point, then, is the firm's residence or center of interest; but this is an elusive and easily misunderstood concept. For our calculations of traffic in the hands of Cuban operators we have rather taken account of the nationality of the firm as a legal person, and, more especially, of that of its owners. Had we focused on the residence, and, particularly, on the "center of interest," the gross freights that one would have to classify as in Cuban hands would be substantially more than those of our estimates.[2]

---

2. The most important omission in our estimate are the gross freights received by the firm operating the ferries and sea trains. For balance of payments purposes there is little doubt about the Cuban character of this firm. Among the reasons for this are its legal status, its tax status, and the residence of its owner. It handles Cuban freight and uses a large

The I.M.F.'s *Manual* in Table V takes account of the following items: (*a*) gross freights, (*b*) expenditures in ports, and (*c*) miscellaneous expenditures. Gross freights are received for carrying exports and imports. For imports they exclude transport costs incurred after customs declaration. Under port expenditures, ships' repairs (but not their conversions, which are considered commodity transactions) are included, as are fuel, food, general ships' stores, port charges, and expenditures of the crews. Among other or miscellaneous expenditures the *Manual* counts the payments of national operators for the chartering of foreign ships or vice versa and the so-called transit expenditures, such as pier charges, loading and unloading costs, commissions, and taxes.

The Results of the Method in the Cuban Case

To calculate Cuba's balance of international payments on ocean transport account, we have used the method of the I.M.F. *Manual.* We have tried to state in some detail the

proportion of Cuban factors of production, including crews and other personnel. Part of its profits have been reinvested in Cuba. In addition, its "center of decisions" is in Cuba and the economic decisions of the firm are made on the basis of the requirements, opportunities, and advantages of the national economy, which determines its growth and which it serves.

If we corrected this omission, which involves considerable gross freights, we would have to make major alterations both on the credit and on the debit side of our balance of international payments on ocean traffic account.

That in spite of the preceding arguments we have opted against the inclusion of this item in our calculations is based on the consideration that this firm offers such a specialized service, and is so different in organization, equipment, costs, and market from the sector that we are interested in here, namely that of freighters, that its inclusion would have obscured that sector's main features. But we repeat that for balance of payments' purposes as well as for some others, the national character of this enterprise must be taken into account.

treatment of particular items and therefore do not merely show the tabulated data, ordered according to the Fund's system. Rather, we have preferred to trace through, step by step, the actual operations performed. Not to have done so would have deprived of pertinent information anyone interested in particular details, and would have left him with doubts about

TABLE 12
Cuba's Balance of International Payments
on Ocean Transport Account:
Credits, 1956

Gross freights for exports*			$ 9,272,660
Expenditures in port			4,005,724
Repairs		$ 100,000	
Miscellaneous supplies		175,000	
Port fees		3,320,724	
Crews' expenditures		210,000	
Fuel		200,000	
Miscellaneous			25,509,433
Pier		12,089,809	
Imports	$11,779,824		
Exports	309,985		
Unloading of imports		3,141,286	
Stowage of exports		7,944,371	
Sugar	7,474,696		
Other merchandise	469,675		
Commissions on sugar freights		414,429	
Consignment fees		150,000	
Tax on sugar freights, 2.75%		1,769,538	
TOTAL			$38,787,817

* Gross freights for imports are not included because all gross import freight receipts by national operators from importers residing in Cuba are payments among residents and have no place on the balance of international payments. In 1956 such freight receipts amounted to $15,411,750. This note has two purposes: to clarify the concept and to underline the importance of the share of Cuba's shipping enterprises in total gross import freights. The total in 1956 amounted to $71,402,411. The sum of $15,411,750 is also important in that it determines part of the values that are given in detail under *Expenditures in port* and *Miscellaneous*, in Table 13.

Note: See pages 111–22 for discussion of figures.

the approach taken; at the same time it would have prevented him from suggesting better alternatives. And improvements are certainly possible; we can in no way pretend that our methods are perfect or even that they yield more than mere approximations to the truth. Moreover, our estimates refer to only one year, 1956, and eventually someone might well want to make similar calculations for earlier or later years. Having available a detailed account of how we proceeded here might then perhaps be useful, at least to help judge some particular items.

TABLE 13
Cuba's Balance of International Payments
on Ocean Transport Account:
Debits, 1956

Gross freights for imports			$55,990,661
Expenditures in port			2,474,733
Repairs		$ 400,000	
Miscellaneous supplies		28,000	
Port fees		659,090	
Crews' expenditures		30,000	
Fuel		1,357,643	
Miscellaneous			10,382,750
Charter of vessels		2,832,000	
Pier		1,663,823	
Imports	$1,534,801		
Exports	129,022		
Stowage		2,248,792	
Unloading		2,024,647	
Sugar exports	1,837,500		
Other exports	187,147		
Commissions		1,613,488	
On imports		1,348,528	
U.S. agency	$1,155,881		
Broker	192,647		
On sugar		264,960	
"Address"	105,984		
U.S. agency	105,984		
Shipper	52,992		
TOTAL			$68,848,144

Note: See pages 111–22 for discussion of figures.

This restriction of the estimates to the year 1956 must, incidentally, be kept firmly in mind by the reader who wants to draw conclusions over and beyond those contained in this book. In 1956 the world's ocean freight market was extraordinarily prosperous and not at all representative of "normal" business conditions. Any argument built on data for that year must therefore necessarily be interpreted as subject to very particular assumptions which should be stated clearly. We have therefore added some data for 1957 and 1958, which might, up to a point, help us put the 1956 figures into perspective and arrive at a somewhat more balanced judgment.

Tables 12 and 13 present the pertinent overall data on revenues and expenditures. The following detailed account of how each item was arrived at makes itemized comments redundant. Nevertheless, a general statement about the interrelation and compatibility of the two tables is in order.

Indeed, it should be stressed that both tables must be viewed and studied together. For instance, it is obvious that as gross export freight receipts—or gross import freights received by Cuban operators—varied, so would certain expenditures. If this variation in freight receipts were positive, a variation in the same direction would occur in the expenditures made in port and in those classified as miscellaneous. The same would be true if we started with an increase of gross freight payments; port and miscellaneous receipts would then also rise. The extent of this can be illustrated by an extreme case. Under the assumption that no Cuban operators at all exist, the following process would occur: On the credit side, port and miscellaneous receipts would go up, while on the debit side all expenditures for the same items would disappear. Thereby total debits (which would only include gross freight payments) would rise from \$68,848,144 to \$71,402,411, which is our estimate of total import freights. On the credit side, gross freight receipts would disappear and the other items (except, of course, ships' charters, which, however, were already calculated at zero) would go up enough to prevent a decline of more than two or three millions in the total of $38,787,817. This would occur in years in which profits in the shipping business were as high as in 1956; in other years, with similar costs and traffic volumes, freight payments would be smaller. Alternatively, costs might rise and gross freights might remain the same; in either case the difference between total credits and total debits on the balance of payments on ocean transport account would be reduced.

All this will be understood more clearly when we analyze the role of Cuban shipping concerns in creating national income. *Given the present structure of Cuba's maritime economy,* they can only do this in two ways: through the remuneration of Cuban crews (including food and lodging aboard ship) and through whatever profits they may earn from their operations. These profits will be estimated for 1956, but we may anticipate that the fact that they were positive in that year does not imply that this is the unalterable rule; in 1957, for example, they were probably nonexistent, or the firms in question experienced losses.

That the basic difference in having the international ocean transport service rendered by foreign or by Cuban operators lies in the net pay of the crews—because they will either be Cubans or foreigners—and in the sign and amount of the firms' net income is the central point to keep in mind when the possibilities and advantages of a national merchant fleet are considered. It is true that the balance of labor income, defined broadly, will always be in Cuba's favor [3] and will add to

3. A part of the pay and maintenance of Cuban crews on Cuban vessels will also appear on the debit side of the balance of payments. This happens to the extent that these crews spend their pay in foreign ports or that the operators purchase their supply of food there. Besides, the substitution of Cuban ships for vessels manned by foreign crews will decrease the expenditures of these crews, as well as the food purchases of foreign operators, in Cuban ports. The net balance in favor of Cuba will therefore be smaller than it might appear at first sight. The multiplier effect on the national income, of the wage payments in question, will therefore also be small.

the respective item in the national income. But the net income of firms can either add to or subtract from the national accounts, depending on whether profits or losses have been made. If the latter occurs, it is an open question whether the positive effects of crews' wages will be greater, equal, or smaller than the negative ones of business income.

Below we will spell out in detail the procedures used to estimate the individual items and sub-items in Cuba's balance of international payments on ocean transport account. We will begin with gross import freights paid to Cuban as well as foreign operators, and with gross exports freights obtained by domestic firms. While what Cuban firms receive for carrying imports does not belong on the balance of payments, it is still very important to know the amount. After the discussion of the calculations of freight bills, the remaining items will be analyzed.

Once again we note that our estimates are only first approximations and that more than at quantitative accuracy we aim at a general qualitative realism.

The Estimation of Gross Freights:
Import and Export Freights

In Table 14 we show the results of our estimates of import freight payments in domestic currency (pesos). Physical volumes are expressed in metric tons.

The data on tonnages, broken down according to whether the freight originated in the United States or elsewhere and according to whether it consists of dry or liquid cargoes, are the same as those used in Table 1. The only additional distinction is that for dry cargo we have discriminated between imports into Havana and those to all other ports. The reason for this further classification, aside from its intrinsic interest, is that we have much more complete information on freights paid in Havana for dry cargo imports from the United States than for the remaining ports.

With respect to the valuation of gross freights, the following procedure was adopted:

1. For liquid cargo the rate chosen was $2 per ton. The validity of this figure is doubtful and cannot really be proven. It is quite probable that a figure closer to $3 or even more might have been better.

2. For dry cargoes shipped from the United States to Havana, gross freights have been computed on the basis of the tonnages registered by forty-three United States ports of origin in *El Avisador*. The rates were there estimated, by ports, according to the composition of the cargoes.

3. For dry cargo imports from the United States into other Cuban ports an average freight rate of $25 was used.

4. The same $25 per ton rate was used for dry cargo imports from the rest of the world.

Although the figures obtained by this rather laborious process may not be exact, they were calculated and checked with

TABLE 14

Estimated Import Freights,
1956

	Liquid cargo	Dry cargo		Total
		Havana	Other ports	
United States				
Metric tons	621,748	1,339,828	441,354	2,422,930
Value (pesos)	1,243,496	37,969,647	11,033,850	50,246,993
Other countries				
Metric tons	1,523,709	509,012	215,308	2,248,029
Value (pesos)	3,047,418	12,725,300	5,382,700	21,155,418
Total				
Metric tons	2,145,457	1,868,840	656,662	4,670,959
Value (pesos)	4,290,914	50,694,947	16,416,550	71,402,411

great care. It is worth noting that the total for gross import freights ($71,402,411) exceeds the official estimate of the Ministry of Finance ($65,964,788) by $5,437,623. We may have used too high an average freight rate for imports not originating in the United States, although this is doubtful in view of the 1956 boom in the world freight market. On the basis of revised import data we have also used a tonnage figure (4,670,959) which exceeds the Ministry's (4,637,279) by 33,680 metric tons. It is therefore possible that part of the difference between the Ministry's estimate of gross import freights and ours, derives from the discrepancy in the tonnage used. Furthermore, the possibility exists that some of the Ministry's freight calculations are f.i.o. (i.e., free in and out, or free of loading and unloading), which would make them smaller than our calculations of gross freights. In any event, we prefer our figures for a number of reasons, not the least among which is the fact that our estimates are much more detailed than those of the Ministry.

Next, it was necessary to estimate the share of Cuban shipping firms in the total of gross import freights in 1956, since this share has to be excluded from the balance of payments. The following procedure was adopted. First, all liquid cargoes were imputed to foreign operators; while this may not be absolutely correct, it is probably not far from the truth. Dry cargo from outside the United States was also assumed to be carried only by foreign firms, although this assumption requires two qualifications. For one, there are occasional shipments, especially some on time-charter vessels handed over by their owners abroad—mainly in Europe—and which then may bring cargoes to Cuba that have to be imputed to the Cuban operator. The other qualification refers to imports carried by Cuban operators from Mexico and Central America. Neither exception could be taken account of, since the necessary data were not available, but together, in 1956, they cannot have amounted to more than 10,000 tons.

Finally, regarding Cuban imports from forty-three United

States ports, we found that twenty-two of these were serviced by Cuban operators. Since we know with considerable accuracy the itineraries and routes of the firms involved, the part of the year in which they operated in 1956, the total traffic on these routes and that in the hands of Cuban firms—562,198 metric tons in 1956—as well as the average freight rate, the estimate of national gross freights which we derived from this information should at least be tolerably correct.

Having then excluded the gross import freights received by national firms from the total, the item entitled *Gross freights for imports* in Table 13, Cuba's balance of international payments on ocean transport account, shows the receipts of foreign shipping enterprises from gross import freights.

Gross freights paid to national firms for carrying Cuban exports were calculated only for raw and refined sugar and a few specific commodities, among which fresh and canned fruits and vegetables, tobacco, sea foods, and rope, plus a variety of smaller items, are the main ones. Other exports, such as molasses and minerals, were not included, although Cuban operators share in this traffic to a certain extent. And our calculations refer only to exports to the United States; those to other countries, especially to Mexico, had to be omitted because their magnitude could not be ascertained.

The receipts of Cuban shipping concerns from gross export freights, shown in Table 12, almost all correspond to the transportation of raw and refined sugar, which amounted to 875,000 tons; only 26,065 tons of other merchandise were involved.

Estimate of the Remaining Items on Cuba's Balance of International Payments on Ocean Transport Account

To show clearly how the remaining headings were calculated, we will first discuss each credit item and then do the same on the debit side. Since in many cases the same basic data underlie the calculations of receipts as of expenditures, this is not the most succinct way of presenting the material, but brevity in this case might cause a certain confusion.

RECEIPTS

Revenues from port and miscellaneous expenditures were calculated for Table 12 in the following manner:

Repairs. This item is restricted to repairs made on ships of foreign operators in Cuban docks or yards. This is simply our own estimate, and the true figure may be several times larger.

Miscellaneous supplies. These are the supplies and provisions purchased in Cuba for the vessels of foreign firms. It was assumed that some 3500 such ships entered Cuban ports in 1956 and that their average expenditure under this heading was $50. Both figures must be regarded as conservative.

Port fees. These include the disbursements made for vessels of foreign operators for such items as dockage, pilotage, and mooring in Cuban ports. The calculations were made on the basis of $0.40 per ton for 4,708,761 metric tons of imports and of $0.25 per ton for 6,708,878 metric tons of exports. Liquid cargoes were included in both cases.

Crews' expenditures. These refer to the purchases made in Cuban ports by the crews of foreign-operated ships. The estimate is based on 3500 vessels staying in port for an average of two days with 20 crew members whose average expenditure is $1.50 per day per head. All assumptions may be considered conservative.

Fuel. Here are included the fuel purchases of foreign-operated ships which had to supply themselves in Cuba because of emergency situations, or because their routes did not take them to cheaper sources of supply. The correct figure may be somewhat higher than the rounded-off total shown.

Ships' charter. These represent the receipts of Cuban operators who rent their vessels to foreign firms. Probably some transactions of this type occur under voyage charters, but none under time charters. Lacking data, the item was left blank; it is not likely to be substantial.

Pier. This includes handling and receiving or delivering—as the case may be—of dry cargo in Cuban terminals, if the merchandise was transported by foreign operators. For imports, $11,779,824, the 562,198 tons shipped by Cuban operators were subtracted from the total cargo imports (2,525,502 tons) and an average cost of $6 per ton was applied to the remaining 1,963,304 tons.

For exports, only 120,000 tons were considered, and from these the 26,065 tons carried by Cuban firms were subtracted. An average pier cost of $3.30 per ton was used for the 93,935 tons left. These exports are mainly fresh fruits and vegetables, tobacco, and miscellaneous merchandise. Molasses, minerals, and some others had to be excluded for lack of data. Since sugar exports are free at shipside (f.a.s.), pier charges are not included in the bill.

Unloading of imports. This item is calculated at an average cost of $1.60 per ton for the 1,963,304 tons of dry cargo imported on foreign-operated vessels.

Stowage of exports. This corresponds to the loading of dry cargo on the ships of foreign enterprises. Sugar is computed at $1.68 per ton for 4,449,224 metric tons. Under *Other merchandise* only the 93,935 tons already mentioned in the discussion of pier costs have been reckoned, at a unit cost of $5.50 per ton.

Commission on sugar freight. Cuban receipts under this heading have been calculated as one-half of the 1.25 per cent commission paid by foreign shipping firms to the shippers of sugar. The assumption is that national brokers or traders account for half of the shipments. The cargoes transported on foreign-operated vessels to the United States were calculated at a freight rate of $9.69 per ton for 1,880,485 metric tons, yielding a freight bill of $18,221,900, of which 0.625 per cent would be $113,887. Sugar exports to the rest of the world in 1956 were 2,568,738 metric tons, all of it in foreign-operated vessels. The average freight rate has been set at $18 [4] per ton, so that 0.625 per cent of the total bill of $46,257,284 amounts to $300,542.

Consignment fees. This item was calculated on the assumption that some 2,000 foreign-operated ships were attended in Cuban ports by national consignees, that half of them paid an average of $100 each in consignment fees and that the corresponding figure for the other half was $50. The resulting figure is certainly much too low.

2.75 per cent tax on sugar freights. The tax rate was applied to total gross freight receipts of foreign shipping firms for sugar exports to the United States and to the total f.i.o. freight bill for sugar exports to the rest of the world, since the latter are carried exclusively by foreign firms. The method of arriving at these freights was described under commissions on sugar freights. It is possible that the tax on sugar exports to the United States may have been overestimated, since some of these shipments may have been contracted on an f.i.o. basis. Since in that case they would exclude stowage and unloading costs, the base to which the tax rate should be applied would be lower than the one we used. However, this difference is not important and may well be offset by cases in which sugar freight shipments to the rest of the world were contracted on a gross basis.

EXPENDITURES

We now pass to an account of the calculations used for the several port and miscellaneous expenditures listed on the debit side of the balance of payments.

Repairs. Represents repairs made in foreign docks and shipyards on vessels owned and operated by national firms, either

4. Free of loading and unloading (f.i.o.), which is the customary form for sugar freight contracts in the world market.

under the Cuban or a foreign flag. The number of such ships was put at ten and the average repair bill of each at $40,000.

Miscellaneous supplies. Purchases of food and other supplies for ships owned and operated by Cuban firms, at an average of $70 for the four hundred times that these ships were estimated to have entered foreign ports.

Port fees. Paid in United States ports by the vessels of Cuban firms. Calculated at $0.60 per ton for the 562,198 tons of imports transported on these ships, $0.35 per ton for sugar exports, and $0.60 per ton for other exports.

Crews' expenditures. Those made abroad by Cuban crews of the ten ships belonging to national concerns. These ships were supposed to have an average crew of 25 men, to have entered foreign ports four hundred times for two days, and to have produced expenditures of $1.50 per day per man.

Fuel. Purchased abroad by Cuban-operated ships. In 1956 all such fuel was assumed to have been bought in United States Eastern Seaboard and Gulf of Mexico ports, where it is cheaper than in Cuba and where it is available all along the routes travelled by these ships. However, it is possible that some fuel was actually bought in Cuban ports. The total bill depends on a number of variables; among them are the number of vessels, length and duration of voyages, number of days spent in port, and sundry conditions under which the voyages took place. Since we could not possibly get accurate information on all these elements, it seemed preferable to use a representative sample. This led to the conclusion that fuel costs on these ships can be estimated at about 5.5 per cent of gross freights.

Ships' charter. More details will be given on this item further on. It was calculated on the basis of (*a*) the number of foreign vessels chartered by Cuban firms, (*b*) their approximate monthly rent, and (*c*) the length of time for which they were under charter in 1956.

Pier. Includes the cost of handling and receiving or delivering—as the case may be—in foreign (United States) terminals, cargoes transported by Cuban firms. For imports, the calculation was made at $2.73 per ton for the 562,198 metric tons brought to Cuba by national operators. For exports, only the 26,065 tons transported in the second half of 1956 by one Cuban firm on the Havana–New York and Havana–Baltimore runs were included. The unit cost used was $4.95 per ton.

Stowage in the United States. Only refers to the 562,198 tons imported in 1956 on vessels operated by Cuban firms. Loading costs in the United States were put at $4 per ton.

Unloading. The unloading abroad of exports transported by Cuban operators. For sugar, the cost was calculated at $2.10 per ton on 875,000 tons, while for other exports, only the 26,065 tons already mentioned were considered, at a unit cost of $7.18 per ton.

Commissions. Paid to foreigners by Cuban operators in payment for services connected with soliciting and handling of freight. The largest commission goes to the United States agency and customarily amounts to 7.50 per cent of gross import freights. Brokers' commissions, which, also by force of tradition, amount of 1.25 per cent of the same freights, are not —as in the case of the United States agent—paid directly to firms doing business with the Cuban operator. Rather, the operator deposits the sums in question with the United States agents of the Cuban importers of the merchandise. It is clearly understood that these agents or forwarders can channel the freight to any of the operators competing on the route, and although this is not always so, the collection of the commission has even become their legal right.

Commissions on gross sugar freight are of three types. The so-called address commission is received by the foreign agent or correspondent of the Cuban sugar trader or shipper, and amounts to 1.25 per cent of the freight. The foreign agent of the Cuban shipping operator also receives 1.25 per cent of the freight. Finally, the commission of the Cuban sugar trader or shipper usually also is 1.25 per cent of the freight. Of this latter commission, it was assumed that half of the sugar transported on Cuban-operated vessels was shipped by Cuban brokers or traders. Since the other half was assumed to correspond to foreign shippers, it was computed as a sub-item among the debits that must be included in Cuba's balance of international payments on ocean transport account.

Cuba's National Income and the Transportation of Ocean Freight: Cuban Maritime Firms in 1956

Having estimated the approximate balance of payments effect of ocean freight transportation in Cuba, we can now turn to the calculation of what for macroeconomic purposes is the most important unknown: the impact of ocean freight transportation on national income or product. In the process we will also be able to highlight some of the major features of the income and expenditure (cost) structure of different sectors of Cuba's maritime industry. This is interesting not only for its microeconomic aspects, but also for determining the behavior of the balance of payments in relation to ocean freight transportation.

Viewed in overall terms, it might be superfluous to stress how important the contribution of sea transport is to our national income; evidently for a country like Cuba a good maritime freight service is indispensable. There are, as yet, no systematic studies of the role of this industry in economic development, i.e., in the growth of national income, of underdeveloped countries. (Professor Daniel Marx, Jr., was engaged in such a study at the time of the writing of this book,[5] but was unfortunately forced to abandon it because of ill health at that particular time.) But the facts shown so far should suffice

5. For the announcement of this, see *The Review of Economics and Statistics,* Vol. XL, Supplement, February 1958, Number 1, Part 2, p. 42n.

to demonstrate beyond question that in Cuba an adequate service already exists, both with respect to the number of routes, ships, and firms and with respect to the stability of the service, and taking into account the favorable geo-economic location of the island. Nor can an adverse impression emerge from our analysis of freight rates; on the contrary, given the market structure of the import and export trades, the opposite conclusion seems plausible.

But in the present context our main interest is not the over-all or generic importance of ocean freight transportation for the national income at large; rather it is the specific contribution made to the national income by the activities of Cuban maritime firms. We will therefore have to study the economic results of their business in detail, and will do so by presenting a consolidated profit and loss statement for the whole industry for 1956. Although this involves a long—perhaps excessively long—digression, some additional points of interest will also receive attention by means of this procedure.

The figures of Table 15 are estimates; just as in the case of the previous tables, we do not claim that they are perfect. Again it is the qualitative aspect on which we wish to concentrate, even though, neither before nor now, do we try to ignore the quantitative implications of the data. The account of how the computations were performed will give a measure of the degree of reliability of the figures.

Expenditures are grouped under three main headings: those derived from freight handling broadly defined; those inherent in the operation of ships; and, finally, general expenditures. The first category, beside pier, stowage, and unloading, includes freight commissions and the 2.75 per cent tax on sugar freights, as well as port fees. Although the last item really pertains to the vessels themselves, it is usual, both in Cuba and the United States, to incorporate it under this heading.

Regarding the second heading, the expenses arising from the operation of vessels are the ones of most direct concern to the operator. Indeed, when freights are contracted on a net or f.i.o. (free of loading and unloading) basis, these expenditures become the only ones that really affect him. Their composition is self-explanatory except for a few items; thus, the amount for "prompt dispatch" is the discount given by the operator to the shipper when he manages to load and dispatch the vessel before the agreed date; should the deadline be exceeded, the user would have to pay a demurrage penalty. These practices are particularly common in the transportation of sugar.

TABLE 15
Estimated Consolidated Profit and Loss Statement
of Cuba's Maritime Firms, 1956

Gross receipts			$24,684,410
Import freights	$15,411,750		
Sugar export freights	8,478,750		
Sundry other export freights	793,910		
Expenditures for freight handling		$14,700,331	
Imports	9,768,049		
Sugar exports	4,383,618		
Sundry other exports	548,664		
Gross receipts minus expenditures for freight handling			9,984,079
Expenditures for the operation of vessels		6,919,089	
Time charters	2,832,000		
Self-owned ships	1,495,225		
Lost time, overtime, claims, prompt dispatch, extra insurance	1,234,221		
Fuel	1,357,643		
Gross receipts minus operating costs			3,064,990
General expenditures		1,234,221	
NET PROFIT			$1,830,769

Finally, general expenditures include the costs of office personnel, professional fees, communications, statistics, advertising, and, in general, the broad range of similar expenditures that is common to all firms, although their composition may vary from business to business.

The procedures used to compute gross receipts have already been explained in the course of the discussion of gross import freights received by national operators and of gross freights for exports as a balance of payment credit. While the calculation of expenditures for freight handling could also be studied on the basis of the discussion of the corresponding balance of payments items, in this case a few summary presentations may be useful. They will also allow us to distinguish in each case between expenditures made in Cuba and abroad (United States).

We shall begin with the import traffic of 562,198 metric tons in 1956. One noteworthy fact is the importance of these costs,

TABLE 16
Expenditures for the Handling of Imported Freight

	Rate	Cost	
In Cuba			
Port fees	$0.40 per ton	$ 224,879	
Unloading	$1.60 per ton	899,407	
Pier	$6.00 per ton	3,372,088	
Total			$4,496,374
In the United States			
Port fees	$0.60 per ton	$ 237,201	
Pier	$2.73 per ton	1,534,801	
Stowage	$4.00 per ton	2,248,792	
Agency	7.50% of freight	1,150,881	
Total			5,271,675
Grand total			$9,768,049

shown in Table 16, in the total cost of the service, since they amount to 63.38 per cent of gross import freights. Expenditures made in Cuba are little more than 46 per cent of total handling costs and about 20 per cent of gross freights.

As for the 875,000 tons of sugar exports in 1956, for which

an average freight rate of $9.69 per ton and a total freight bill of $8,478,750 was calculated, their handling costs are shown in

TABLE 17
Expenditures for the Handling of Sugar Exports

	Rate		
In Cuba			
Port fees	$0.24 per ton	$ 218,750	
Stowage	$1.68 per ton	1,470,000	
Shippers' commissions	0.625% of freight	42,992	
Tax	2.75% of freight	233,166	
Total			$1,974,908
In the United States			
Port fees	$0.35 per ton	$ 306,250	
Unloading	$2.10 per ton	1,837,500	
"Address" commissions	1.25% of freight	105,984	
Agents' commissions	1.25% of freight	105,984	
Shippers' commissions	0.625% of freight	52,992	
Total			2,408,710
Grand total			$4,383,618

Table 17. Sugar handling charges were 51.70 per cent of gross freights; 45.05 per cent of the handling costs were incurred in Cuba and this represented 23.30 per cent of gross freights.

The commissions of shippers were divided equally between Cuba and the United States, so as to keep this calculation compatible with that of the balance of payments. Actually, since all these commissions, as well as the 2.75 per cent tax, are computed on the basis of handling charges plus all other cost components of gross freights, they should not really be assigned fully to handling charges. Following the usual accounting practice here, however, saves us from the need to split this item repeatedly under different headings, even though it is not an ideal solution.

Finally, Table 18 shows the breakdown of the handling charges for the 26,065 metric tons of sundry non-sugar exports, for which at an average rate of $30.45 per ton a total freight

TABLE 18
Expenditures for the Handling of Sundry (Non-Sugar) Exports

	Rate per ton	Cost	
In Cuba			
Port fees	$0.25	$ 6,516	
Pier	3.30	80,015	
Stowage	5.00	130,325	
Total			$216,856
In the United States			
Port fees	$0.60	$ 15,639	
Unloading	7.18	187,147	
Pier	4.75	129,022	
Total			331,808
Grand total			$548,664

bill of $793,910 was calculated. The expenditures shown represent 69.10 per cent of the corresponding gross freights; 49 per cent of the expenditures, or little more than 27 per cent of the gross freights, are incurred in Cuba.

A recapitulation of the proportions in question shows to what extent handling charges account for the cost of the service rendered by Cuban shipping operators. They are somewhat more than 50 per cent for sugar exports, over 60 per cent for general imports and almost 70 per cent in the case of the goods typical for the Havana–New York route. Both costs and prices determine, at any given moment, the relation between the three proportions. For example, as already explained, there is no doubt that the handling of sugar is easier, faster, and less risky than the handling of a representative sample of imports. Similarly, since the exports from Havana to New York contain a high proportion of fresh fruits and vegetables, they require much special attention. Besides, the longshoremen who have to work in refrigeration chambers draw special pay, which in turn raises costs. On the price (rate) side, the fluctuations in sugar freight rates, together with the relative stability of its handling cost, make the share of the latter particularly volatile. We have seen what it was in 1956, when freight rates were high; after they slumped in 1957, the share of handling costs rose greatly. By way of contrast, on the import side and in the case of "general" exports, conference freight rates as well as handling charges are very stable; consequently the share of the latter in the total freight bill shows few changes over relatively long periods.

The share of total freight handling costs that is spent in Cuba varies between 40 per cent for general exports and 45 per cent for sugar exports and for imports. The greater efficiency of operations in the United States explains the difference, since it results in shorter stays in port. Needless to say, compared to other pursuits in Cuba, the average level of pay among port personnel is rather high.

Returning to the expenses of operating vessels, the payments for time charters by Cuban operators were calculated by putting the number of ships chartered in 1956 at thirteen, eleven of them at an average monthly rent of $18,000 each, and the other two at $38,000 each. The estimate is probably a conservative one.

The operating expenses of Cuban-owned vessels, including the four state-owned "Bahia" ships, are detailed in Table 19.

TABLE 19
Estimated Operating Expenses of Ships Owned by
Cuban Maritime Firms in 1956

Payroll of ten vessels	$ 540,000
Food	155,125
Repairs, dry dock, maintenance, etc.	400,000
Insurance	200,000
Depreciation	200,000
Total	$1,495,125

With reference to the figures in this table, it was stated above under *Crews' Expenditures* (p. 120) that an average crew of 25 men per ship was assumed, so that a total of 250 men is involved. The monthly payroll per ship, including social benefits, is $4500,[6] and the daily upkeep of the crew $1.70 per man, which may be on the high side. Items like repairs, dock costs, maintenance, and insurance do not present any special difficulty, but the same is not true for depreciation. If it were based on the resale value of the ships, which in 1956 amounted to an average of $500,000 per boat, the annual depreciation charge would have to be very high, since most of the vessels are quite old. The figure chosen, $200,000, would in fact imply a further 25-year lifespan for the ten vessels valued at $5,000,000, if the depreciation is made at 4 per cent per annum. This assumption clearly is unrealistic to the point of absurdity; nevertheless $200,000 may not be too far from the firms' actual accounting practices.

The figure for fuel on the consolidated profit and loss statement of the Cuban maritime industry was already explained under *Fuel* in the discussion of the balance of international payments. In 1956 it had to be high because diesel as well as fuel oil was priced well above the 1954 and 1955 levels, especially in the last months of the year. Prices reached their peak in February, 1957, and fell markedly thereafter.

The item that includes lost time, overtime, claims, prompt dispatch, extra insurance, etc., and the one for general expenses were calculated by assuming that together they might amount to 5 per cent of gross freights. Depending on the type of freight carried, some firms might exceed and others not reach this proportion, but the net error of the estimate cannot be large.

The calculation of the gross freight receipts and the subtraction of the various expenditures lead us to net profits as the residual item. Other considerations about them will be presented further on; here we restrict ourselves to noting that under Cuba's present economic structure and that of the na-

6. Since the crews of the four "Bahia" ships were both larger and better paid than is normal, we may have underestimated this item.

tional maritime industry, the contribution of the latter to the national income is, for all intents and purposes, restricted to the payrolls—plus upkeep [7]—of the Cuban crews of Cuban-owned ships and to the profits of Cuban shipping operators.

The Remuneration of Crews and the Transportation of Ocean Freight

If the direct contribution of Cuban operators to the national income consists in the wages that they pay to their Cuban crew members and in their profits, it is important to inquire into the magnitude of these payrolls when compared to the tonnages moved and the freight payments received. It will also be interesting to see by what factors such a relation is determined. Along these lines we hope to gain a deeper understanding of some of the features that are most peculiar to Cuba's maritime economy and whose relevance is becoming increasingly obvious.

Specifically, we will now try to answer the following question: What proportions of the total cost of the transport service, or of Cuba's gross maritime freight receipts, are the payrolls of ships manned by Cubans? The answer will, in turn, lead us to an explanation of the variability of these proportions as well as why, given the present traffic structure, either proportion must necessarily be small. Both for exports and for imports we can base the present analysis on the data and conclusions of the preceding chapter.

Beginning with exports, consider the data of Table 6 pertaining to the composition of the costs of transporting sugar from Nuevitas to Baltimore and returning in ballast. The round trip was said to take fourteen days. Its payroll, broadly de-

7. No monetary value can be calculated for lodging, since no market price exists. As for the foreign crews of chartered vessels, it must be recorded that six of these ships were—and are—mainly manned by Cubans.

fined, i.e., including basic wages, supplementary pay, and upkeep), was 4.30 cents per 100 lbs., or 10.8 per cent of the
total costs of 39.72 cents per 100 lbs. In the example of Table 7,
when it was assumed that instead of returning in ballast the
ship would carry fertilizer, the travelling time imputed to sugar
was reduced to ten days. Crew costs then become 3.08 cents
per 100 lbs., and the so-called costs of the voyage also fall
slightly, because some of the port expenditures in Baltimore
now can be imputed to the transportation of fertilizer and also
because the lower freight bill will in turn reduce the commissions paid on it. What must be stressed is that the length of
the voyage has been reduced by four days so that the costs
of the vessel have declined proportionally, but that expenditures for the loading, unloading, and handling of sugar have
remained practically unchanged. This is why, when the voyage
becomes shorter and the payroll cost falls to 3.08 cents per 100
lbs. of sugar, it represents only 9.2 per cent of the total costs of
33.47 cents per 100 lbs. The greater the reduction of the
duration of the voyage, the more would the ratio of ship's
costs to total transport costs fall and the greater would the
share of port and freight handling costs become. Equally, the
longer the voyage takes, the higher a proportion of total transport costs are the costs of the vessel and the smaller will be
the relative weight of freight handling charges. Therefore, if we
assume that the relative share of other ships' costs is constant,
we may conclude that the costs of crews rise and fall with the
duration of the voyage, but that in either direction they vary
proportionally more than total costs.

To confirm this further, suppose that sugar must be transported from Nuevitas to some imaginary port which would
imply a 42-day round trip, or one three times as long as
that to and from Baltimore. The costs of the vessel would
triple; instead of 17.25 cents per 100 lbs. they would be 51.75
cents. Suppose further that freight costs (except commissions
on freights, which would of course have to rise proportionally)

remain unchanged, so that total transport costs rise from 39.72 to about 75 cents per 100 lbs. Crew costs having risen three-fold, they will be 12.90 cents per 100 lbs. instead of 4.30 cents; thus they will become 17.2 per cent of the total transport cost. The importance of labor costs, then, is closely related to the distance between the ports serviced.

Although our illustrations referred only to the transport costs of exporting sugar, the same point can be made for the costs and gross freight bills of transporting imports. Distance is equally important in that case, but the share of labor costs in total transport costs or in gross freights declines. The reason for this is simply that, while return trips are likely to have about the same duration as the outgoing ones, so that the costs of the vessel may not differ much, handling and port charges are usually much higher (see Table 11) for imports than for sugar exports. If total costs or gross freights for imports were, on the average, only two to three times as high as those for sugar exports, the percentage of labor costs in these totals would of course only be between 3 and 5 per cent.

The above examples illustrate a vital fact about the possibilities of increasing the national income by means of labor income generated by Cuba's ocean traffic. Since this traffic primarily takes place between Cuba and the Atlantic Coast and Gulf of Mexico regions of the United States, the distances to be covered are inevitably short, as must therefore be the duration of the voyages. Costs of the vessel are therefore a correspondingly small proportion of gross freights or of total costs which consist primarily of port and freight handling charges.

It follows that crew costs, too, must be a small proportion of total costs and of gross freights. It need hardly be added that if vessels manned by Cuban crews could travel to much more distant ports, the share of labor income in gross freights would rise. But this possibility is restricted by the imbalance between the volume of freight available for exports to and imports from countries other than the United States. This imbalance makes it very difficult to establish efficient and profitable services on routes whose main feature must be very long voyages.

One clarification, however, is in order. It must be clearly understood that the preceding analysis is based on the figures of our Tables 6 and 7 which describe the so-called costs of the vessel. Among these are two items which, while by no means arbitrary, may not always represent reality accurately. They are the depreciation (20 years) and interest charges (6 per cent) on a new vessel bought with borrowed money at one million pesos or dollars. The figures for depreciation were, we repeat, not arrived at capriciously. They reflect the prevailing world market quotations of the last few years and the usual prudent practices of ships' owners,[8] although these may vary. The interest rate, too, is the one normally used in Cuba for loans involving the purchase of ships. But even so, it is also true that a substantial part of Cuba's ocean traffic could be serviced by vessels with lower depreciation and interest charges, and even by already fully depreciated ones (if the twenty-year rule is adhered to), whose capital cost is not calculated on a resale basis. In that case the share of crews' costs would be somewhat larger except to the extent that insurance, repairs, maintenance, and fuel might also be costlier on older vessels, as is indeed probable.

A Digression on Cuba's Maritime Economy in 1957–1958

Our analysis of the significance of Cuba's maritime economy for the balance of payments and national income was necessarily limited to 1956 data. It is therefore somewhat static and would undoubtedly be more interesting if longer periods could be considered. Then longer-term structural changes as well as

8. At present, operators often use depreciation periods of fifteen years or even less.

cyclical fluctuations of Cuba's export and import freight markets could be examined, and, if such a dynamic approach were feasible, it would certainly merit another chapter. But even though a study of so wide a scope is not possible at this time, some additional information, however fragmentary, may be of interest when it is concerned with a subject as little studied as Cuba's international ocean traffic. We therefore present below a few additional notes and comments on the events of 1957 and 1958 in Cuba's maritime economy, although they are too incomplete to warrant a separate chapter.

There is no doubt that in 1957 the share of national operators in Cuba's international freight traffic increased. Although exact figures are not yet available, it seems quite safe to assert that instead of 875,000 metric tons of sugar as in 1956, these operators seem to have shipped at least 1,200,000 tons to the United States, and probably close to 50 per cent of all sugar exports to that destination. On the important New York–Havana route, Cuban operators commanded 52.7 per cent of the traffic, a figure that will rise further in 1958, and on the Baltimore–Havana run their share was 55.1 per cent. On most other routes on which Cuban firms had been active in 1956—sometimes with up to 100 per cent of the traffic in their hands—their share did not decline. And the Havana–New York freight was almost completely in Cuban hands after one firm in mid-1956 ceased being a foreign enterprise.

What were the reasons for this very respectable overall growth in the traffic volume transported by national firms? To answer this question, let us consider once more the profits item of Table 15, since it seems reasonable to assume that, among other factors to be listed below, high profits were a stimulus to the expansion.

Profits of the national industry in 1956 were estimated at $1,830,769. They may actually have been somewhat larger, since one debit sub-item may have been overvalued; one firm during part of 1956 did not use a United States agent but had its own foreign office and therefore need not have paid the agency commission of 7.50 per cent on gross freights. The foreign office's expenses were not considered in the consolidated income and expenditure statement of the industry. However this probably is of slight importance, as are also some other adjustments that could be made on the debit side. By and large, therefore, our calculation of profits seems to be fairly accurate.

As a proportion of gross freight receipts these profits were 7.42 per cent. At first glance this might seem a satisfactory but not an extraordinary profit when compared to those of other industries during boom periods. But when we consider that the capital invested by Cuban operators may at the time not have exceeded seven or eight million pesos, the 1956 results look excellent. While these profits by themselves were not enough to provoke the expansion we are trying to explain, there were other contributing factors that help account for it. In the first place, it seems likely that reasonable profits had already been earned in 1955, which would have helped financially and psychologically to create an expansionist environment. Secondly, during the second half—and particularly in the last months—of 1956, the outlook seemed increasingly promising as the world freight market began to boom under the impact of the Suez affair. The demand for sugar seemed to point to large quantities, high prices, and very high freight rates. The sugar boom itself, together with other factors, seemed to augur an unprecedented increase in Cuba's national income in 1957, with expected imports correspondingly high. Prices of ships, both new and second hand, had been rising, especially since the last quarter of 1954; given the continued rise in the price of steel and other materials and of wages in shipyards, together with the general expectation of more inflation, conditions seemed to indicate a continuation of this trend. Everything seemed to argue for the need to ensure one's supply of shipping space, be it by purchase or by charter, with the former generally preferred because of the state of expectations. More-

over, public and semi-public institutions made a singular contribution to the speculative boom by extending substantial
credit facilities that were channelled to this industry which is
always intensely attractive to persons with a bent for gambling.

It is also probable that as a result of the rather juicy profits,
which must have meant a high degree of utilization of their
capacity, a certain sense of euphoria and carelessness may
have begun to pervade the older and more established enterprises. They may therefore not have guarded with their usual
diligence against the entry of new rivals or the growth of
insignificant ones. This lowering of the traditional firms' vigilance gave infiltrators, as Pareto would have said, a perfect
chance to *vivoter*.

The 1957 expansion of Cuban shipping concerns took several
forms. One firm, Naviera Garcia, in mid-1956 had already
acquired the organization, facilities, and time-charter contracts
of the Ward Line, an important foreign firm. Other firms
added about four ships to the fleet owned outright. By means
of quasi-public credits, six ships were acquired, one of them
for a producer of fertilizer and the other five for charter by
two firms newly created for this purpose. And, finally, the fleet
operated by Cuban firms under time-charter was increased by
four or five units. Although not all the ships mentioned were
available throughout the whole of 1957, there evidently was a
considerable expansion.

The short- and medium-term expectations referred to proved
to be totally mistaken. Table 20 shows the degree of the col-
lapse of the international maritime market. It was due to several factors, among which two predominate:

> *a*) a reduction in the volume of world trade in some com-
> modities; this was particularly violent for coal, which
> accounts for over 50 per cent of all the world's tramp
> traffic;

> *b*) an extraordinary increase in the tonnage of freighters
> available on the world market.

Table 20 shows the tonnages of ships contracted for tramp service in 1956 and 1957 as well as in the first quarters of 1957 and 1958. In the breakdown of the main cargoes contracted for, the sharp decline of the demand for vessels to carry coal

TABLE 20
Total Contracts of Tramp Vessels for the
Transportation of Particular Products
(thousands of tons)

	Year 1956	Year 1957	1st Quarter 1957	1st Quarter 1958
Coal	48,341	38,523	19,270	2,596
Cereals	17,751	14,115	3,546	4,045
Scrap iron	3,717	3,174	1,028	251
Minerals	5,681	9,322	2,512	1,359
Sugar	2,122	2,766	884	644
Chemicals and fertilizers	2,583	3,134	794	1,027
Wood	705	1,170	152	338
Miscellaneous	2,313	3,530	515	897
Total	82,213	75,734	28,701	11,157

Source: *Westinform Shipping Report* No. 107, April 1958.

stands out. These contracts represent new operations planned, and are therefore more representative of market trends than the traffic actually taking place at the time. As for the availability of ships, the world's merchant fleet amounts to a total of about 110,000,000 tons gross register. Freighters and passenger boats (a little more than 30,000 units) comprise about 80,000,000 tons and tankers (almost 4000 units) with almost 30,000,000 gross register tons. The growth in the last few years has been tremendous, and data on planned launchings permit the prediction that it will continue for some time to come. Over 30,000,000 additional tons are either under construction at present or have been contracted to be built; 70 per cent of this represents tankers and the rest largely freighters. The volume of tankers under construction, the equivalent of 70 per cent of the world's present tanker fleet, is evidently impressive, but so is the addition of 16 to 18 per cent of present capacity represented by the freighters under construction. Even an intensive scrapping of old ships during the next few years would not possibly offset this new tonnage which, moreover, will consist of more modern vessels whose voyages and port operations will be speedier. For the time being, and until world trade recovers vigorously, millions of tons of freighter capacity will lie idle.[9]

For Cuban operators the 1957 decline in freight rates had serious repercussions in the sugar sector, especially for the firms that had more vessels in the second half of the year, when the rate slump became spectacular. The increase in the number of firms and ships sharpened competition for general cargoes, export and import, and excess capacity rose while rates in this line hardly varied.

Costs, on the other hand, increased. The unloading of sugar in United States ports became costlier. Fuel prices declined after having reached their highest levels since 1951, but only by mid-December were they back to where they had been in October, 1956. Repairs, insurance, and other smaller items went up. And the increase in the number of ships of the national fleet produced competitive bidding among the Cuban firms for crews to man the new vessels.

Firms operating with chartered vessels suffered the sharpest immediate blow, since most of their charters, valid for 1957 and part of 1958, had been contracted at the peak prices prevailing in the second half of 1956 and the subsequent three or four months. Table 21 shows levels of time-charter contracts for the vessels most representative of the Cuba–United States traffic.

One glance reveals the gyrations of the time-charter market for ships suitable for the transport of Cuban sugar between the beginning of 1956 and the middle of 1958. After a rise in the first quarter of 1956, prices levelled off until fall. Then

9. By mid-1958 the total tonnage of idle vessels was equivalent to about 7 per cent of the world's merchant fleet.

the Suez affair produced a renewed increase until April of 1957, after which prices fell, well into 1958, reaching levels which would seem to preclude the possibility of further declines. These data cover ships of about 3400–3600 deadweight tons, most of them being of 3500 tons. This limitation prevents a larger and more continuous number of observations but makes for the greatest possible comparability. Even so, differences still exist, since in spite of their similar tonnages the ships may differ widely in speed, cubic capacity, kind and amount of fuel consumption, loading equipment, distribution of holds, age, place of delivery by the owner and return by the charterers, etc. The length of the charter contract is another im-

TABLE 21
Time-Charter Quotations of Representative Vessels

	Deadweight tonnage	Monthly payment	Pesos per deadweight ton	Length of contract (months)
1956				
January	3,500	$24,500	7.0000	9–12
February	3,500	25,750	7.2534	12
March	3,500	26,750	7.6428	10
August	3,545	27,125	7.6510	12
September	3,600	28,000	7.7777	7
November	3,350	29,500	8.3100	11–13
1957				
January	3,500	31,000	8.8571	12
April	3,550	32,250	9.0842	12
November	3,420	15,000	4.3860	9
December	3,600	14,500	4.0277	6
1958				
February	3,543	12,500	3.5280	12
May	3,615	12,000	3.3195	6–7

Source: Maritime Research Inc.

portant variable which interacts with the general market picture and the particular situations of individual owners and charterers at any given time. But even with all these qualifications we can accept the series as representative; its general configuration is confirmed by the parallel course taken by the prices for larger and smaller vessels at the same time, namely by ships in the 1500 to 6000 ton range. These are the outer limits of what may be considered a handy size for the traffic in question and when the market makes it advantageous, operators will switch to ships lying in this general range. In other words, when the prices of "ideal" sized ships begin to appear excessive to an operator, he will begin to shop for ships that are still adequate, even though in particular features—tonnage or freight capacity, for example—they may be less desirable. Similarly, when the time-charter market is so depressed as to permit the charterers more generous profit margins within certain limits, they may contract for somewhat larger ships than usual. This, of course, will also largely depend on the state of freight rates, sugar freight rates in Cuba's case.

Table 22 shows that the movements of quotations for *Cimavi*-type vessels were roughly analogous to those of ships between 3400 and 3600 deadweight tons. Theoretically at least, *Cimavi* ships are completely uniform, having been constructed as a homogeneous series. Since their displacement capacity is 6000 tons deadweight, they constitute the upper limit of ships used for the Cuba–United States run.

Our data on time charters leave no room for doubt about the increased costs which Cuban operators experienced on this account in 1957. It is the most important cost-item; adding the other cost increases mentioned and comparing them with freight receipts, which were poor in the second half of the year, and especially those derived from sugar, it becomes indisputable that the profits of firms operating with chartered vessels must have been negligible or negative.

The position of operators who owned their vessels cannot have been too good either, particularly if they purchased new units at the end of 1956 or in early 1957. The market slump made it difficult or impossible for them to meet their interest and amortization charges out of current income. Furthermore, the world-wide decline in freight rates also brought with it a severe drop in the prices of second-hand vessels, so that the resale of these ships at present would represent major losses.

TABLE 22
Time-Charter Quotations of *Cimavi* Ships

	Monthly payments	Pesos per deadweight ton	Length of contract (months)
1956			
February	$32,500	5.4167	24
March	32,500	5.4167	15–17
August	42,000	7.0000	4½
November	42,500	7.0834	4
1957			
March	47,000	7.8334	4
May	43,500	7.2500	4
June	31,500	5.2500	3
July	28,850	4.8083	22
August	28,500	4.7500	12
1958			
February	20,000	3.3333	11
May	16,000	2.6667	12

Source: Maritime Research Inc.

When the depressed maritime market showed no signs of quick recovery, some firms went into liquidation. If other things remain the same, among the survivors those who operate with chartered vessels and who can replace their present high charters quickly with contracts more representative of present market conditions will have the best chance of overcoming the crisis. Those who operate their own vessels probably will find their yields affected for a long time by the reduced capacity to adjust to cyclical changes in the maritime market. Both types of firms will do their best to contain the incursions of competitors which have already managed to offset some increases in conference rates agreed upon in late 1957 or early 1958. These increases may either be regarded as a delayed response to the preceding cost increases, or as an attempt to compensate for the declines in other freight rates, especially for sugar. Perhaps both factors operated simultaneously and the second may have strengthened the first. In any event, the overall market situation prevented the general implementation of the increases.

The shortness of the period studied makes valid conclusions about cost and freight rate behaviors impossible and thus also precludes conclusions about the course of profits through the maritime business cycle. But it seems likely that profits per unit rise rapidly in the first phases of expansion, begin to decline as the peak is approached, and fall steeply as the contraction begins. These results would seem to be very similar to those Arthur F. Burns believed to be applicable to the railroads of the United States.[10]

Be this as it may, we believe that the preceding discussion of post-1956 developments in Cuba's maritime freight transporting firms should make it possible to deduce with considerable accuracy the sign and amount of these firms' direct contributions to the balance of payments and national income in 1957. Although in that year the enterprises in question expanded their operations greatly, they were seriously affected by the sharp and sudden decline of the world freight market. They may suffer from the effects for a long time.

10. "Railroads and the Business Cycle," in *The Frontiers of Economic Knowledge* (Princeton: Princeton University Press, 1954), p. 205.

5

THE PROBLEM OF A NATIONAL MERCHANT MARINE

W HAT HAS BEEN SAID so far will give at least a general indication of the basic economics of the problem of a national merchant marine. The purpose of the present chapter is to offer an overall view of the matter in the light of the material previously dealt with, adding some further details and leading to an integrated analysis of the whole issue.

Though highly interesting, the theme is a difficult one to deal with, because of its sentimental and emotional connotations. To treat it objectively means to focus sharply on the difference between what intuitively might be felt to be the impact of a merchant marine on the national economy, and what, in the light of the known facts, it can be estimated really to be.

It is the illusion of greatness that springs from seeing one's national flag waving from the mast of an ocean-going ship that in the final analysis accounts for the almost universal, a priori, acceptance of the importance of having a national merchant fleet. Common to all nations, this attitude cannot in itself be criticized; it is after all no more than an expression of patriotic sentiments. But patriotism aside, an economic analysis of the question must necessarily take into account a series of very different considerations. And that means that whoever undertakes such a task, inevitably runs the risk of having to play the unpopular role of a kill-joy. But the world is already too filled with confusions and fallacies that often, under the guise of more or less elaborate sophisms, do little more than pander to the egotism of individuals or groups. Economists, in particular, can testify to the truth of this, nor is the general public ignorant of it.

In fairness it must be said that public opinion in Cuba has not yet been *manipulated*, by those interested in the development of a national merchant fleet, to the same extent as it has been in other countries in which such propaganda reaches unimaginable volumes and costs. Even allowing for the differences in size, the case of the United States is notorious in this respect. According to its present economic structure, the United States is not a maritime nation; both by employment and by value of production, ship building and operating ranks rather low on the industrial scale. Nevertheless, on the one hand "its vociferous lobbyists wage an unceasing campaign for Congressional and executive attention" and on the other, "the voluminous official records of hearings, exhibits, reports, and legislation silently attest to their success." [1] The United States example is particularly blatant, but by no means unique; merchant fleets have often been the most fertile field for the most exaggerated protectional chauvinism.

Merchant Marines and Military Preparedness

If we can strip away the layers of emotion that all too often cover up the special vested interests involved, we must still ask ourselves whether persuasive arguments can be found in favor of policies designed to develop national merchant marines. Such arguments have always been fundamentally of a dual character: military and mercantile or economic. Their traditional connection was epitomized in Goethe's well-known

1. Wytze Gorter, *United States Merchant Marine Policies: Some International Economic Implications* (Princeton University, Essays in International Finance, No. 23, June, 1955), p. 1.

phrase "Commerce, war and piracy: inseparable trinity." To dominate the seas has in the past been the key to trade, and the English saying that trade follows the flag, embodies this relation. Today, however, there is little truth left in it; in a world in which the balance of power has changed so drastically in a few decades, it is not so strange that some causal relations may also have been reversed so that at present it is traffic potential that promotes navigation services, rather than the reverse. This is not to deny that once a certain service has been initiated with a certain minimum volume of freight, the service itself may create increasingly favorable conditions for a further trade expansion.

At present then, the undoubted former importance of sea power as a stimulus to merchant fleets no longer exists. Their relation is different—if not reversed—and it is no longer the development of trade that counts, but general strategy in times of war. Indeed, for large powers the availability of an ample supply of freighters has been a major factor in times of armed conflict since it has enabled them to move the necessary supplies to their armies and civilian populations. The experience of World War II bore this out fully, and it is this experience that is still being used as the main argument to defend the policies by which inefficient merchant fleets are protected in some countries. But in this greatest war of our generation, the impact of nuclear science only made itself felt at the very end. Its later developments, and particularly its military applications, seem to upset all prior postulates of military strategy. Today two alternatives exist: one may either accept the optimistic hypothesis that the destructive power of existing and future weapons will prevent the upset of the unstable duopolistic balance of power, so that coexistence or, better still, universal understanding, may result. Or one may start from the premise that the outbreak of any new war will be sudden and that such a war cannot continue for long enough to produce the complete immolation of mankind. In either case the employment of national merchant marines for military ends would largely be excluded; even under the second, catastrophic, alternative, there would be no time to move the supplies needed for a prolonged conflict. Based on this reasoning, an expert in the economics of ocean transportation, Wytze Gorter, of the University of California, questions the validity of the military argument, which is being used as the *ultima ratio* by the propagandists of the industry in the United States.[2]

He does, however, admit some other possibilities. One is that however brief a future world war might be, it could still be so destructive that the postwar reconstruction would require the mobilization of enormous volumes of materials and equipment. For this, plentiful shipping would be advantageous. At this level of speculation, such an eventuality is not at all absurd; nor need one rule out another, namely, that in the course of the so-called cold war emergency situations which might unsettle the international shipping market may arise at the far corners of the globe. The great powers, therefore, for reasons of high—if that is the word—policy might still find it desirable to assure themselves of ample cargo shipping capacity. Of course, as the author also notes, this does not necessarily mean that such a fleet must be built or maintained by the United States itself. Other countries, tied to the United States by mutual defense agreements, would seem to be better suited to this role, both because of their economic structure and because of their naval tradition.[3]

As for Cuba, the argument can be disposed of briefly. It is quite true that some advantage may accrue to the country from the possession of its own merchant fleet in the early stage of a conflict. Later on, however, it is equally probable that the tonnage available for Cuba would be determined in the context of overall priorities set by the countries with which Cuba

2. Wytze Gorter, *United States Shipping Policy* (New York: Harper & Bros., 1956), pp. 6–10 and 73–78.

3. *Ibid.*, pp. 103–5 and 118–20.

has international alliances. Among many other reasons, the importance of sugar makes it extremely likely that within this group, Cuba would receive fairly substantial allocations.

The Economic Significance of a Merchant Marine

If in this day and age the military role of merchant fleets is no longer to *conquer* markets, economic justifications of policies protecting national shipping industries would have to be based on other grounds. If considerations of prestige are ruled out, what remains are questions of alternative opportunities to improve the structure, and raise the yield, of the economy. In short, what matters is the impact of such a policy on the composition and level of the national product and, secondarily, on the balance of payments, although in fact these two priorities are often treated in the wrong order.

With respect to their impact on the national income, one will have to distinguish direct from indirect effects and take into account the adequacy or insufficiency of a country's international maritime transport services. By indirect effects we mean, as noted previously, the overall impact on an economy of having its supply of transport facilities in balance with its traffic potential; direct effects are the income flows originating in freight-carrying activities themselves, and which are recorded in the computation of national income and product by their industrial origin. In turn, whether or not a country has available an efficient ocean transportation service for its exports and imports is a weighty factor in deciding how far a fleet development policy should be carried.

Viewed in this way, it becomes apparent that when a country can already count on an efficient ocean transport service, the indirect effects on national income are already occurring. The direct effects, on the other hand, will depend on the degree of national participation in this service. In any event, the least favorable situation would be the one in which the service is unsatisfactory and the national participation in it is minimal. Finally, there can exist merchant fleets that not only carry a large share of their country's trade, but also participate actively in the trade between other countries. In the latter case, of which important examples exist, both the indirect and the direct effects of the shipping industry on the national income are greatest.

The availability of an efficient service depends primarily on whether or not attractive payloads exist and on whether a country's geo-economic location is favorable. In the absence of protectionist policies, the degree of participation of national fleets in this service or in that between other countries depends on the structure of the economy. The question is whether either a country's endowment of natural resources or its man-made conditions make this activity a more suitable source of employment of its factors of production than any alternative productive activity. The relative abundance or scarcity of the resources needed to develop a merchant marine—particularly the special skills acquired over time—explains the changing maritime fortunes of nations. Great Britain is a case in point; its maritime tradition and experience were already of long standing before the introduction of iron ships moved by steam. When these vessels came into common use, the United Kingdom found itself with a great advantage over other countries in gaining a leading position in this industry. With abundant iron and coal it had the prerequisites to make the steel as well as supply the fuel for its ships, and it had in addition an invaluable store of nautical knowledge, trained crews, and a world position of renown both economically and politically. With such decisive advantages there was nothing surprising about the rise of its merchant marine, its shipyards, ports, and schools of navigation. Nor should we wonder at the strength and multiplicity of its private shipping enterprises and of the many auxiliary concerns in brokerage, insurance, etc. It was the abundance of appropriate natural and human resources that, by being efficiently utilized with increasing specialization, permitted cumulatively rising additions to the national income. For Britain the merchant marine represented an industry in which it possessed a distinct comparative advantage and, hence, one in which productivity could be maximized.

If the British case is an example of optimum utilization of given natural, human, and technical resources in a maritime industry, other countries that have tried to develop their fleets have found that, even without such a favorable factor endowment, the industry may offer more productive employment to labor and capital than do the available alternatives. If arable land and other natural resources are in short supply, and if a long acquaintance with the sea already exists, a growing population in need of work may well find that offering international ocean transport services to the world may be a better source of income than other activities. Norway is a notable example.[4]

These nations are only two outstanding examples of the relationship between the basic economic structures of countries and the development of commercial shipping. Sometimes this nexus is extremely strong and sometimes it is more tenuous, but even in the latter case a country's possibilities of participating in any degree in this traffic will in some way be influenced by the structure of its national economy or by factors derived from this structure. Thus, local operators usually tend to have an advantage over foreign-based shipping concerns, since they are better able to maintain close contacts with the users of the service and to act in accordance with the true needs of their market. Particularly on oligopolistic routes, given equal rates and services, the national enterprise may often receive some preferential consideration from local shippers simply through the good personal relations maintained by its managers or sales corps. And, more important still, it is likely to have

4. Over 85 per cent of Norway's carrying capacity is employed exclusively for voyages between foreign ports.

more up to date information on traffic flows and on the non-market forces that may affect these flows at any time.

Since the basic principles and assumptions underlying the economics of merchant marines, and the effects of the latter on the national income and the balance of payments, have now been covered, we might pass immediately to their application to the Cuban case, so as to evaluate the desirability of a national fleet development policy. There is, however, one other relevant issue that is rarely dealt with, but the pertinence of which will become obvious shortly, namely, the long-term trend of freight rates on the world market. Rate fluctuations also deserve some special attention; only when these two topics have been studied will we have a complete framework for the complex issue of the development of national fleets.

Trends and Fluctuations of Freight Rates and the Development of Merchant Marines

It would seem obvious that, when the desirability of any particular project is analyzed within the framework of an over-all development plan, not only the short- and medium-term outlook is taken into account, but also those longer-run tendencies that are commonly called secular trends. We will state without attempt at proof that this is not always necessary for individual firms; for them the short and medium run may be by far the most relevant period within which to shape price and production policies.

But when the problem is to modify significantly the structure of magnitude of an economy, such long-term projections are not merely interesting but vital. Policies designed for this end are macroeconomic and have numerous repercussions; more important still, they imply the decision to use vast resources in one particular line and to divert them from others. It is therefore necessary to obtain as accurate a picture as possible of the more remote future for the various alternative lines of activity that might be developed with the available resources.

In the considerations of the advantages and drawbacks of a policy designed to foster a national commercial fleet, then, the long-term prospects of the industry are of vital significance. Therefore, even inconclusive data and deductions about what the future may hold for the international maritime economy deserve attention to the extent that, within the prevailing uncertainty, they help us make a judgment. If what appears to be the secular trend of the past is projected into the future, conditions do not appear to be very favorable for countries that want to develop national fleets without already possessing a solid naval tradition.

Reference has already been made to Daniel Marx, Jr.'s, *International Shipping Cartels.* In that work the author studies international freight rate quotations between 1873 and 1937, for both tramps and regular lines.[5] Although he cautions the reader about the limitations of the data, which are based on a study by V. D. Wickizer[6] and do not reflect such factors as improvements in ship construction, increases in speed, and changes in the composition and direction of trade, a trend does seem to emerge for the period studied.

Using the tramp index as being representative also of regular line freight rates—naturally only as a first approximation— Marx finds a steady decline until 1908, although wars produced occasional small deviations from this trend. Moreover, freight rates fell by more than the general wholesale price index and the process continued for about ten years longer than for the general index. After reaching astronomic levels during World War I, rates again declined uninterruptedly until 1937. For this period, too, Dr. Wickizer concludes that, compared to the general price level, freight rates were continuing their tendency to decline.

These findings cover the period between 1873 and 1937.

5. *International Shipping Cartels,* p. 242.
6. V. D. Wickizer, *Shipping and Freight Rates in the Overseas Grain Trade* ("Wheat Studies of the Food Research Institute," Vol. XV, No. 2, 1938), and Daniel Marx, Jr., *International Shipping Cartels,* p. 26.

For subsequent decades the following facts stand out. Although World War II raised rates appreciably, they fell far short of the levels reached during World War I. And in the postwar period the prevailing tendency was again downward; only the Korean conflict and the Suez affair produced some brief interruptions. It is illustrative of the extent of the deterioration that the rate for shipping cereals from North Atlantic ports of the United States to Le Havre (France), which in 1948 was about $3.75 per ton,[7] was in June of 1958 not even $3.50 a ton, in spite of the increases in costs experienced by shipping operators in the meantime.[8]

Although Marx and Wickizer do not, themselves, offer an explanation for the observed secular deterioration in world freight rates, it is quite possible to attempt such an explanation in terms of conventional economic theory.

One may argue, for instance, that probably both the supply and the demand operating in this market have become progressively less elastic. Thus, on the supply side several reasons for this may be adduced:

1. Countries for which the sea offers a *natural* field of employment of their resources—particularly of their labor—tend to expand their naval activities. Some of

7. Marx, *International Shipping Cartels*, p. 243.

8. Difficulties in obtaining reliable data have prevented the author from concluding the study he had under way, in which he attempted to compare sugar freight rates with f.o.b. prices. The hypothesis may however be advanced that probably the secular deterioration of rates would also be confirmed in this respect. To verify this one would have to compare sugar price series with net freight rates, i.e., freight rates minus loading and unloading charges. For sugar prices we have those of Cuban raw sugar in New York, including cost and freight, from 1900 on. To calculate net freight rates, we have data on gross rates for some years before World War II and for approximately the last ten years. To convert these figures into net rates, we would at least need a good deal of unavailable information on port handling costs. Even so, unless the available figures contain major errors, it would be found that in 1937, for instance, freight rates for Cuban sugar shipped to New York averaged 22 cents per 100 lbs. (data supplied by Willet & Grey and by Luis Mendoza y Cia. and published in the *Cuban Sugar Yearbook*, 1939,

these countries have virtually no known economic alternatives.

2. Countries without a natural maritime bent have pursued increasingly nationalistic and protectionist policies to develop their own fleets. The United States is a spectacular illustration of this phenomenon, which has helped depress the markets of traditional maritime nations.

3. Ships generally are undifferentiated goods, although substantial efforts are made to produce some differentiation. Such efforts consist in specialized construction for particular cargoes (fuels, minerals, fresh fruits and vegetables), but even so, when overall freight rates are depressed, the impact of differentiation declines. At present, for instance, petroleum tankers are being more frequently offered to transport cereals. Despite all attempts to separate markets, the fact is that substantial declines in certain freight rates tend to filter to the whole industry; with such a homogeneous product, then, prices can well be explained in terms of present value theory.

p. 65), while loading charges in a Cuban north-coast port were 1.890 cents per 100 lbs. But at the time of writing this text the freight rate is 34 cents per 100 lbs. between a Cuban North Coast port and a United States port north of Cape Hatteras. This is an increase of 50 per cent over 1937; loading charges, on the other hand, are at least 8 cents per 100 lbs., or 400 per cent more than in the prewar year mentioned. Even if we took some other prewar basis for the comparison—1938 or 1939 for example, when gross freight rates were about 15 cents per 100 lbs., so that an increase of 225 per cent would emerge for freights—the rise would be smaller than that of loading charges. It is also probable that unloading costs in the United States rose greatly during this period, so that nominal net freight rates may at present be about equal to their prewar level, while in real terms they would have declined.

It is to be hoped that careful research will eventually produce conclusive results on this point, so that in the future the first impression that has been recorded in this note will be either confirmed or corrected.

On the demand side the possibility of decreasing elasticity is suggested by the fact that certain users—government agencies among them—have acquired dominant positions and, thus, command now at least partial monopsonic or oligopsonic power.

Some of the previous considerations are rather close to those employed to maintain the thesis of Prebisch and Singer of secularly declining terms of trade for countries producing primary commodities. If we could be sure that our facts and our theory are correct, and if what we have suggested were firmly established, namely, that on the long run freight rates tend to fall relative to the prices of the goods transported, it would mean that to encourage the development of merchant marines in underdeveloped countries would be to urge the allocation of scarce resources toward the production of a service for which the market is becoming increasingly inelastic. Worse, it would imply using increasing amounts of scarce capital to build fleets instead of using the most *abundant* factors of production—land and labor—to produce and process primary products. This would be totally contrary to economic diversification, which aims precisely to produce more *differentiated* products for which demand is generally more elastic. In the case of Cuba it would mean that in the attempt to diminish the dependence on sugar—which offers poor prospects for national economic development because the demand for it is so inelastic—we would develop an activity with market characteristics similar or worse.

These considerations highlight the theoretical and practical importance for underdeveloped countries desirous of fostering merchant fleets to make exhaustive inquiries into the long-term trends in international ocean shipping markets. Such an inquiry would also be linked to other studies needed to pinpoint the true significance of such a policy; particularly a comparison between the cyclical fluctuations of freight rates and the overall cycles experienced by underdeveloped countries would be of interest. Such studies would deepen our understanding of what general and sectoral targets we should actually aim for, and what would be the most appropriate tools for their achievement.

We have referred to cyclical fluctuations only in passing, but there is no doubt that they, too, merit special study, with particular attention to the problems of primary-commodity-producing countries and of very open economies. Such economies are particularly dependent on an efficient freight transport service; if for any reason—such as an unfavorable geo-economic location—they should lack an adequate service, and if a thorough investigation confirms such a diagnosis, there may be a good case for a policy designed to overcome all the usual obstacles to non-spontaneous developments and to create a national merchant marine. But when a country located on the periphery of the market for its primary commodities finds, as does Cuba, that its export and import needs are attended to by excellent ocean transport services, the obstacles that would be encountered by an attempt to develop a domestic shipping industry must weigh much more heavily. Policies in which costs will exceed benefits must be avoided, and in such a calculus the impact of cyclical fluctuations in freight rates is an important variable.

Primary products themselves, with their inelastic market conditions, are subject to frequent and serious price and production fluctuations. Stabilizing one or the other—or income received from them, employment created by them, or all of these and other variables simultaneously—is a major concern of countries producing such commodities. General economic stabilization becomes the more difficult, the larger the share of a particular commodity in the national product and in the foreign trade is. Diversification is therefore considered as an escape from the excessive dependence on only one line of production, and one faced by inelastic foreign demand, at that. But is it really desirable to pursue such diversification by encouraging an activity as unstable as shipping, with fluctuations that tend to reinforce those of the primary commodities themselves? In Cuba, for instance, maritime freight rate fluctuations do not offset oscillations in the so-called world sugar market (which excludes that of the United States). Rather, when the production and exports of sugar fall and no special compensatory mechanisms are at work, the national income declines, imports follow suit, and so do freight receipts. The latter may happen both because of declining rates or, if rates are fixed, merely because of a smaller volume transported. Therefore instead of neutralizing or mitigating the sugar-induced fluctuations in the Cuban economy, freight receipts evidently act cumulatively on these fluctuations through the nexus between the demand for and price of transportation and the value and volume of cargoes.

It may therefore be concluded that the cyclical as well as the long-term analysis of freight rates must be given prime attention in any plan to develop a national merchant fleet. However, in spite of their demonstrable importance, both aspects could only be treated cursorily in this study; a thorough inquiry along the lines merely sketched here should be given high priority in the future because of the important theoretical and practical issues involved.

The Limitations of Fleet Development Policies

Cuba's foreign trade is presently adequate in size and composition to support the excellent maritime transport service that it receives. This service is of extraordinary efficiency and—as far as sugar exports are concerned—competitiveness. On the import side, although the service is supplied by an oligopolistic market, it is abundant, regular, and geared to the needs of the users. Cuba does not suffer from a lack of transport facilities; if more stable and varied routes than presently exist have not been established, it is for good economic reasons.

In all cases in which the normal payload is adequate to maintain a service, ships are available to supply this service. And for intermittent or sporadic shipments too, it is easy enough to find willing operators; any Cuban rancher who may want to send a partial or a full shipload of cattle to Venezuela—to give a recent example—will find the necessary means. And if he repeats the experiment, he will find—as demonstrated by the example referred to—increasingly favorable conditions of delivery and freight rates, and a service increasingly geared to his particular requirements.

It is therefore no exaggeration to assert that Cuba's present ocean transport service leaves little to be desired in its indirect effects on the national income, along the lines of the previous discussion of such effects.

Concerning the direct effects on the national income, these were already explained as coming from the share of Cuban firms in the country's international freight market. We would venture to argue that, given Cuba's economic structure, much more has already been achieved in this respect than is generally believed, and that there is little ground for the oft-repeated assertions about our backwardness. We also will argue that in consequence of the above, additional efforts to increase this share will either be futile or, at the very least, produce sharply diminishing returns.

Actually, to speak of the development of a Cuban merchant fleet is to have in mind some particular share of total export and import freight revenues for Cuban firms. The proportion aimed for varies, but this author is not acquainted with any contribution to the discussion in which capturing more than half of the total traffic has been deemed feasible; more often, in fact, and somewhat more realistically, 50 per cent of the total traffic with the United States is spoken of. There seems to be no empirical basis at all for this particular figure; instead of a result based on even a minimum of justification, it is rather put forward as a vague *desideratum*. Sometimes, when this proportion is mentioned for trade between Cuba and the United States, it is referred to as if this traffic should be divided between the vessels of both countries—other flags presumably would be excluded—like a pie equally shared by two friends with equal appetites.[9] What is not usually realized is that the actual share of Cuban operators in the Cuba–United States traffic is already close to the 50 per cent mark. In fact, and independent of abstract and theoretical goals, it may be said to be much larger if only the exportation and importation of dry cargo is considered. Table 23 is revealing as far as imports are concerned and deserves a detailed examination.

Above all, it must be noted that the percentage shares shown for 1956 exceed those of 1955 and continued to grow in 1957. Cuban operators, for example, in 1957 accounted for more of the imports from New York; by the mere fact that in mid-1956 one of the existing firms passed into Cuban hands, the total share rose to approximately 53 per cent.

Another important point is that the concern that operates the ferries, which legally and economically may be considered Cuban, carries almost all cargoes from West Palm Beach and thus accounts for about 17 per cent of Havana's total imports. The same firm also maintains a service from New Orleans, and the respective tonnages were not included when the shares of Cuban operators were computed for Table 23.

Finally, concerning the other ports from which Cuban vessels are absent, it will be noticed that those that are very far from our shores, such as ports on the Pacific (Vancouver, Seattle, Tacoma, Portland, Los Angeles, San Francisco) are serviced by ships from other nations, such as Japan, being

9. Perhaps the 50 per cent criterion merely reflects the prevalence of a similar idea in the United States. There it is often thought that the policy of subsidizing the merchant marine implicitly aims at such a share, even though in actual fact a share of less than 25 per cent has been achieved and there are no signs that it is growing.

TABLE 23

Share of Cuban Shipping Concerns in Havana's Imports
from the United States, by Ports of Origin,
1956

Port	Yearly tonnage (metric tons)	Percentage carried by Cuban concerns (estimated)
Albany	51,089	
Astoria	807	
Baltimore	71,500	32
Beaumont	5,229	47
Bellingham	929	
Boston	7,074	
Brownsville	1,402	47
Brunswick	629	
Charleston	27,531	100
Corpus Christi	799	47
Philadelphia	24,756	
Freeport	9,804	
Galveston	7,513	47
Georgetown	4,288	
Gulfport	3,967	
Houston	98,236	47
Jacksonville	1,706	100
Key West	569	
Lake Charles	31,362	
Los Angeles	9,174	
Miami	11,222	40
Mobile	11,101	100
New Orleans	292,715	15
New Bedford	134	
Norfolk	67	50
Newport News	25,468	
New York	264,605	36
Orange	2,528	47
Panama City	816	100
Pensacola	26,474	100
Port Arthur	1,592	47
Port Saint Joe	5,827	100
Portland (Maine)	3,403	
Portland (Oregon)	23,246	
San Francisco	41,544	
Savannah	16,752	100
Seattle	3,138	
Sears Port	1,285	100
Tacoma	1,017	
Tampa	30,354	50
Vancouver	5,945	
West Palm Beach	231,861	
Wilmington	100	100
Total	1,359,828	

Source: Information from Cuban shipping concerns.

ports of call on longer voyages. Since no regular or large Cuban export or import trade with these ports exists, there is nothing that would justify a two-way service. As for other, closer United States ports to which Cuban vessels go only occasionally, the majority are used mainly for bulk merchandise shipments, for which freight rates are usually lower than any other. Besides, this traffic too is irregular and without adequate return freights.

The share of Cuban operators in the imports of other Cuban ports from the United States may be estimated at around 75 per cent, except in the case of Santiago de Cuba, where it is negligible. If the routes between Gulf ports and Puerto Rico were not reserved for United States vessels, Cuban operators might perhaps service them and they could then supply Santiago en route. As it is, however, this port does not offer sufficient attractions for regular services.

There is probably no tendency for a further spontaneous expansion of Cuba's share in the freight market. Conversely, however, there also seems to be no reason why, in the absence of a serious world-wide depression, the share of the Cuban firms should be expected to fall, although the traffic structure is flexible enough to make changes in the relative importance of the different ports possible. In any event, the most important changes in the proportion under consideration come from the transfer of Cuban firms to foreign ownership and vice versa.

On the export side, it is enough to recall that the participation of Cuban shipping firms in the sugar traffic to Gulf ports is close to 50 per cent, and that if sugar shipped from Havana on ferries is included, the figure is even higher. Furthermore, if the operator in the fruits and vegetables shipments is considered Cuban, 100 per cent of this trade is in the hands of national transporters, and the same is true for some other products.

Regarding dry cargo trade with the rest of the world, it can be shown that the composition and imbalance of export and import cargoes and freight receipts, as well as the requirements regarding frequency and regularity of service, militate against greater participation by Cuban operators. With some neighboring countries an incipient service is in the making, and, as payloads improve, Cuban participation may rise in the future, but for the time being the necessary conditions to make this profitable simply do not exist.

The limitations that originate in hard geo-economic facts to curb Cuban participation in its international maritime traffic can be quantified. It is possible to estimate the value of total gross freight receipts and to break this down according to whether it represents trade between Cuba and the United States or between Cuba and the rest of the world. This is done in Table 24.

TABLE 24
Estimated Gross Freight Revenues Originating in
Cuba's Maritime Trade,
1956

	Metric tons	Estimated freight receipts (dollars)
Total trade:		
Exports	7,610,943	98,791,957
Imports	4,670,959	71,402,411
Total	12,281,902	170,194,368
Trade with the United States:		
Exports	4,688,497	39,496,670
Imports	2,422,930	50,246,993
Total	7,111,427	89,743,663
Trade with other countries:		
Exports	2,922,446	59,295,287
Imports	2,248,029	21,155,418
Total	5,170,475	80,450,705

Although the figures in Table 24 are only estimates, it is unlikely that the margin of error is very great. Import freight receipts were calculated according to the method described when analyzing the corresponding balance of payments item.

Export freights, on the other hand, were estimated on the basis of the contracts registered in the 1956 *Yearbook of Maritime Research* and some private information supplied to the author.

One can get a general picture of the overall amounts of freight receipts in Cuba's international maritime trade by combining Tables 1, 14, and 24. The total of export and import freights is high, higher perhaps than is ordinarily realized, although it must be pointed out that cargoes as well as freight rates were above normal in 1956. This was true particularly on the export side; these, as we saw, are mainly shipped by tramps, whose rates fluctuate greatly.

Indeed, the total figure is so large that it may easily stimulate fanciful ideas about the excellent prospects for Cuba's naval development. This would be unrealistic; we have already seen that the above figures are gross and that, if the considerable loading and unloading charges as well as a series of other costs in Cuba and abroad were subtracted from them, even under the extreme assumption that all traffic is carried in Cuban bottoms, only a fraction of the impressive 170,000,-000 pesos would remain as a positive balance.

A breakdown of total trade into that with the United States and that with the rest of the world, shows that, while both figures are substantial, there are certain noteworthy differences between them. Trade with the United States is larger, both in tonnage and in freights paid. Freight rates per ton are, on the average, higher for imports from the United States than from the rest of the world. This is caused partly by the small volume of liquid cargoes, whose rates are low, originating in the United States and partly by other factors, such as the f.o.b. price of the merchandise, the frequency, regularity, and degree of specialization of the service, as well as the handling charges involved. These factors both permit and require high gross freight charges for merchandise from the United States so that the effect of the shorter distance—excepting Pacific

Coast ports—tends to be offset. These factors operate much less strongly in the case of imports from the rest of the world which, moreover, contain a high proportion of liquid cargoes. Thus, although the influence of distance on freight payments is not negligible, it does not turn out to be a factor of decisive importance.

A different picture emerges on the exports side. Traffic to both regions is mainly in cargoes with low unit f.o.b. costs, the service is mostly irregular, and handling charges are not a very costly item. In such a case distance becomes a primary factor, particularly when, as in 1956, ships and rates free of loading and unloading (f.i.o.) reach very high levels. Indeed, the influence of distance is such that even though the tonnage exported to the United States exceeds that going to the rest of the world, freight payments for the latter traffic are the larger of the two. This remains true, even if from the 4,688,497 metric tons exported to the United States we subtract the 1,276,300 metric tons that were liquid cargoes (mainly molasses), which, at an average freight rate of $3 per ton, would represent a total freight charge of $3,838,900. As will be shown below, the reason is the difference in sugar freights. But before returning to this point, we will present a breakdown of Cuba's other exports to both regions.

The United States, beside the liquid cargoes noted above, received another 656,712 metric tons, of which some 120,000 were fruits, vegetables, and a large number of miscellaneous items which paid an average freight rate of about $30 per ton. The remainder of 536,712 tons consists mainly—almost 500,000 tons of it—of minerals. The average freight rate may be about $10 per ton. Non-sugar exports to the rest of the world in 1956 were only 99,822 metric tons of liquid cargoes (molasses and alcohol), which at $5.50 per ton represented a freight bill of $549,021, and 253,886 metric tons of other goods, almost half of them minerals. At an average rate of $20 per ton these involved freight payments of $5,077,720.

Returning to sugar, it may be noted that, in 1956, 2,755,485 metric tons were shipped to the United States and 2,568,-738 to the rest of the world. The average gross freight rate for the former was $9.69 and for the latter $21, a figure obtained by adding three pesos as average loading and unloading costs to the $18 f.i.o. rate used to calculate the commission on sugar freights in Cuba's international balance of payments on transport account, in Table 12. Total freight charges for sugar sent to the United States amounted to $26,700,650, while for the rest of the world they were $53,668,546, even though the tonnage sent to the United States was greater. Although, as noted, in 1956 this phenomenon was particularly pronounced, these figures illustrate how strong the influence of distance is in this trade. When in 1957 and 1958 freight rates slumped, the difference between the two freight bills declined greatly.

We may now recall what was said about the participation of national shipping operators in trade with the United States. It is so high both for imports and for exports that any attempt to increase it further would—even if successful against the existing competition—yield the unpleasant necessity of having to carry freights, particularly on the export side, at hardly remunerative rates.

The advantages and possibilities which the trade with the rest of the world offers to Cuban operators are really non-existent. Imports, other than of liquid cargoes, are small and command low freight rates, beside originating in a large number of countries. And exports, which are primarily raw sugar shipments, go to many different destinations and, at that, often to countries in which no return loads are available. Some examples may suffice to illustrate this. Sugar shipments to Japan in 1956 amounted to 603,807 metric tons and at least 18,000,000 pesos in gross freight charges (based on an estimate of $30 per ton, which may err on the low side). Gross import freights, on the other hand, had to be paid on cargoes valued at only $3,256,000 and must therefore have been comparatively negligible. Similarly, in 1956, 212,634 metric tons of sugar were shipped to the Soviet Union without any imports at all reaching Cuba from that country. In addition, 263,743 metric tons went to a number of Middle and Far Eastern countries (Syria, Lebanon, Israel, Iran, Pakistan, and Ceylon), so that freight payments of at least 7,000,000 pesos must have been made, but the imports originating in these countries were inconsequential. In South America, 46,345 metric tons were shipped to Uruguay, yielding a freight bill of perhaps 1,000,000 pesos; the total value of Cuban imports from the same country was 3000 pesos. Greece and Finland received 41,047 and 26,847 metric tons respectively and in these as in many other cases the most distinctive feature of the return freight is its absence. All illusions regarding the possibility of a vigorous expansion of the Cuban-owned fleet should therefore be abandoned if they are merely based on overall freight bills and tonnage figures. No useful purpose would be served by adding more details; we need only add that even on routes on which some possibilities for a balanced traffic seem to exist—such as the trade between Cuban north-coast ports and some Western European ones—the most careful calculations indicate that only in exceptionally favorable circumstances could they be profitable. The conjunction of necessary favorable factors would include cheap vessels, high freight rates, and the right timing of export and return cargoes. But even under the most favorable assumptions, the profits obtainable could not be compared with those that similar circumstances would yield in the traffic between Cuba and the United States.

An objective appraisal of the facts, then, can lead to only one conclusion. The possibilities of a Cuban merchant marine are severely limited and circumscribed by our geo-economic framework, but, to the extent that they exist, they are already being exploited. Substantial additional growth will only be possible, if, in the course of time, new opportunities appear.

This comparison of what is possible and what is already

being done shows how little a policy of fostering the national merchant fleet would contribute directly to the national income. Some further considerations will bear this out. Let us suppose, for instance, that a target were set to add ten vessels to those already operated by Cuban shipping concerns. Supposing further that all other conditions remained the same, i.e., that the existing enterprises continued with the same number of ships as before and that the volume of traffic and the routes covered remained unchanged; it would inevitably follow that the new ships would not find profitable payloads. But even if, for the sake of argument, we disregarded this fact momentarily, another aspect of the matter should still concern us. If the ten vessels were fairly new and suitable in their design to the requirements of our traffic, their purchase would represent an expenditure of $10,000,000 to $15,000,000. They would employ some 250 crew members with an annual income of perhaps $550,000, plus some $150,000 for their maintenance. This would yield a much lower ratio of labor income to capital than could be obtained with a similar investment in other lines of production in Cuba, where abundant natural resources in a proper combination with capital and labor at least would permit a greater employment effect. Moreover, it is doubtful that even this presumed annual crew income of $700,000 would, on the short run, go wholly to Cuban hands, since there is a considerable shortage of the skills needed for the higher and more responsible positions, and at least a training period would be necessary before the required personnel would be forthcoming.[10]

The direct effect of the ten ships on the national income would be the labor income referred to. Only if the vessels yielded profits would the effect be larger, but unless the world shipping market improves greatly, this is out of the question.

10. For an objective and honest, albeit indirect, analysis of this matter, see Manuel Lagunas Romaguera, "Ventajas y Desventajas del Uso de los Motores Diesel en los Buques Mercantes" ("Advantages and Disadvantages of the Use of Diesel Engines in Merchant Ships") in the journal *Marinos* (Havana, February–March, 1958), pp. 20–26.

Indeed, probably the net losses which the ten ships would produce if the present structure of Cuba's shipping business were maintained would go a long way to offset or even exceed the direct effect of labor's remuneration on the national income.[11]

In actual fact, a further point of the greatest importance is that if these hypothetical ships entered into the Cuban–United States freight market, beside involving economic difficulties for their owners, they would probably upset the economic equilibrium of the existing firms and make their profitability extremely precarious, so that the possibility of widespread economic losses cannot be excluded.

On the basis of the detailed analysis of the preceding chapter, it is easy to trace the effects of all this on Cuba's balance of international payments. To do so here would therefore be superfluous.

The Problem of Shipyards

It may be possible to make some more favorable assumptions about the effects on the balance of payments and the national

11. It might be argued that in the example the national income should also rise because of higher managerial and administrative income in Cuban shipping firms. This is correct, but unless the volume of traffic itself expanded—instead of a mere substitution of domestic for foreign carriers—this effect would be limited to some managerial posts and to only very few, if any, administrative ones. The smallest effect would be produced if a domestic firm bought out a foreign one, since in that case probably one management would run both firms and not only the foreign managers of the purchased firm, but also some Cuban employees, would lose their livelihoods. The argument about the income-raising effects of nationalistic development policies in some branches of economic activity is, evidently, a dangerous one. As for insurance premiums, which directly or—through reinsurance—indirectly are at present paid to foreign firms, they have only a negligible effect on the national income. The same is true for most of the bank credits granted to the domestic shipping industry by quasi-official institutions, especially when the foreign financing obtained by official banks is taken into account.

income of a policy that fosters a national merchant marine. For this we concentrate on the largest item in maritime costs, which is the cost of the ships themselves.

Undoubtedly, for a country that is generally well endowed for maritime activities, an efficient ship building and operating industry can be a very positive factor in its economic development, if it can utilize domestic resources. We have already seen that the case of Great Britain is historically noteworthy in this respect.

Although the relation is not as close and well defined as is sometimes supposed, a connection between the construction and the operation clearly exists. It may, however, not always be easy to establish clear-cut rules as to which of these activities should antecede the other and which one is the prerequisite for the stability and prosperity of the other, so that in practice it may be best that in a given country both activities have a comparative advantage over others. This possibility would not be compatible in theory with full international specialization, since the principle of comparative advantages operates in relative rather than in absolute terms, so that strictly speaking some countries would construct ships, others man and operate them, and perhaps even crews and operators should be of different nationalities. But in reality specialization is not carried that far, and the efficiency of one country in ship construction, when accompanied by an "acceptable" operating cost level, or vice versa, is usually enough for the simultaneous development of both activities. The yield of both together may not differ too much from the theoretical optimum if their differences in efficiency roughly compensate each other. Hence, for a country to operate shipyards and ships simultaneously, either one or the other should be extremely efficient and the other one moderately so. Otherwise, the need for protection of both activities will bring about the sort of difficulties from which the maritime development policy of the United States suffers, where it is just about impossible to establish clearly and consistently what the basic means and ends of the policy are meant to be.

One can hardly pretend that Cuba enjoys special comparative advantages internationally in the operation of ships; the small size of its firms and the high costs of its crews suffice to substantiate this. Thus it seems obvious that a policy to strengthen its maritime activities and to enhance their positive impact on the balance of payments and the national income through the development of shipyards deserves the most careful attention.

Unfortunately the author must plead total ignorance of the economics of naval construction; the following considerations must therefore be regarded as entirely tentative and undogmatic. Only the logic of ordinary economics will be employed to ask whether, given the present structure and industrial development of the economy, investments in shipyards are the most efficient use of scarce capital. Some factual information may support the logic of the question.

In principle there seems to be a consensus that the economic development of a country must tend toward the eventual optimal utilization of the factors of production. This implies that, within the limits set by the state of technology, the most abundant factor must be utilized in the greatest proportion. For the time being and until the unemployment problem is much nearer to a solution, this implies for Cuba that scarce capital should primarily seek out the fields in which a given investment provides the largest number of jobs. It seems reasonable to assert that in general shipyards do not meet this test.

For a definitive analysis, rather than simply an opinion, we should have concrete data on the type of shipyard needed, its approximate costs, the means available for financing it, its ship-building capacity and the tonnage, characteristics and end use of these, its efficiency, vessel construction costs, etc. Nevertheless, even without this needed minimum information, it may be useful to discuss a few points connected with the world-wide outlook of existing shipyards as well as with their effects on employment.

A recent estimate has put the construction capacity of the world's existing shipyards at slightly more than 9,000,000 tons. In other words "the present yard capacity suffices to rebuild the present world fleet every twelve years, although the ordinary life-span of ships is about twice that period." [12]

For the moment, and in the next two years, the present capacity will be used intensively, but beyond 1960 the outlook is not only uncertain, but dark. Aside from order cancellations, as vessels already contracted for reach completion, the competition for new orders will grow, especially if the 1957 slump in the price of materials is not reversed. The competitive position of shipyards in countries with relatively low labor costs and high degrees of efficiency and mechanization like Japan, Italy, and the Netherlands will then become stronger.

The surplus of shipyards and ships, together with the uncertainty as to whether world trade and production will soon

TABLE 25

Approximate Cost of Building a 10,000-Ton Ship
in the United Kingdom

	Materials costs	Labor costs	Total costs
1. Steel plates, casting, iron work, hatch covers, booms, etc.	£161,475	£ 70,605	£232,080
2. Deck machinery and equipment, etc.	92,205	8,455	100,660
3. Installations, pipes, reefer chambers, decks, paintwork, etc.	54,130	57,085	111,215
4. Main and auxiliary engines in engine room, pumps, generators, etc.	225,665	86,355	312,000
5. General expenses, insurance, register and classification fees, profit margin, etc.	—	—	187,300
Total	£533,475	£222,500	£943,255

Source: *The Shipping World* (January 8, 1958), p. 26.

12. *The Shipping World and World Shipbuilding* (London), February 26, 1958, p. 235.

return to the 1955–1957 growth rates, make the future profitability of the ship-building industry very questionable. But even if the outlook suddenly became much brighter, the original question would still stand: Is a shipyard one of the better investment opportunities in Cuba if maximum employment is an important goal? Even without daring to give a categoric answer, we think that the following facts and analytic considerations cast some doubts on any facile affirmative answer.

In the first place it is worth noting that the labor component in the total costs of ship building is not particularly high. Table 25 illustrates this. It describes costs prevailing in British yards in January, 1958. Without going into the characteristics of the ship—which are described in the source—it will be enough to note that labor costs, when strictly defined, accounted for only 23.5 per cent of the total. And to obtain even this much, a very substantial prior investment in the yard itself is required.

Moreover, the question arises as to what the employment generated by operating a shipyard would actually amount to. Would it be significant when compared to the capital invested? We do not have any experience to draw from in Cuba, but data from other countries may help us obtain a general idea of the magnitudes involved. In 1957 West German shipyards built 323 ships of a total of 1,100,000 tons, and employed 103,000 persons. The average numbers of tons and workers per ship were 3,405 and 318, respectively. And in Norway, where, in the first half of 1957, 44 ships with a total displacement capacity of 133,377 tons were built—and at least 200,000 tons for the full year—the number of hands employed in 1956 in the country's 32 shipyards was 14,500, and did not rise subsequently.[13] It may, incidentally, be noted that under the influence of technological advance, an intensive process of eliminating labor requirements is at work in the ship-building industry. Thus in Japan, where labor is relatively cheap, im-

13. See *Información Comercial Española*, (March, 1958), pp. 291–93.

provements in methods, techniques and equipment have in the last eight years produced a 20 per cent saving in the steel utilized, but much more striking is the 50 per cent reduction in labor requirements for a given output.[14]

These figures may not show precisely how many workers might be employed in a Cuban shipyard, but they do create the impression that it could be nowhere near as large a number as is sometimes mentioned.

Furthermore, it is likely that at least for some years a Cuban shipyard would have to employ an even larger proportion of foreign specialized personnel than would be needed later. The effects on the national income and the balance of payments would be correspondingly smaller.

If the benefits that derive from the installation of a shipyard through its impact on the demand for labor are questionable, those attributable to the induced demand for Cuban goods are even smaller. In Table 25 some of the materials and equipments needed to build a ship are listed. Most of them have to be imported into Cuba. Motors especially, which alone represent a somewhat larger item than labor costs, not only need an advanced manufacturing technology, but, for economic reasons, tend to be produced for the whole world by only a few firms. Improvements are constantly made in such machinery, but for this large research expenditures are necessary; only the most industrialized countries can afford these, and even then only with government support.[15] Besides, adequate materials and equipment must be available at all times, since any interruption in their supply would raise construction costs. But to maintain large inventories also is a costly solution.

It might be argued, on the other hand, that a profitable

14. Masso Yamashita, "Asi es la Industria Japonesa Constructora de Buques" ("This is Japan's Ship-Building Industry"), in the journal *Informacion Mercantil Japonesa,* No. 3 (1958), p. 12.

15. See "Government Support for Industry" in *The Shipbuilding World and World Shipbuilding,* May 21, 1958, p. 487.

level of activity in a shipyard does not merely depend on new construction, but also on repair work, especially in times of low building orders. But in Havana the construction of a dry dock is already underway, and its purpose is precisely to do repair work. At least in principle it would seem reasonable to await the experiences that its operation will yield and to see to what degree it will become a training center in naval metalworking before deciding on future shipyards.

Many considerations come to mind about the conditions needed in Cuba to make a shipyard advantageous. They relate to the excess capacity that might have to be borne for the present in order to meet future needs, as well as to the advantages and disadvantages of different locations, both in terms of direct and social costs and in terms of accessibility, particularly for repair work. But these will not be analyzed here; rather they should remain the concern of whatever specialists will eventually make a full study of the matter. But in general, and in view of the present structure of the Cuban economy, there do not seem to be sufficient reasons to suppose that the inclusion of shipyards in a Cuban maritime development program would significantly benefit the national income or the balance of payments.

Fuel is another item which, in spite of its negligible importance for the national income and the balance of payments, is of some magnitude in absolute terms. Cuban shipping operators usually purchase their fuel in the United States, which turns out to be cheaper than getting it in Cuba, although they have to sacrifice some of their carrying capacity for the return trip. Since there are refineries in Cuba and since the fuel in question can be considered a by-product, it is possible that oligopolistic market practices contribute—together with fiscal or tariff reasons—to the present price structure. But this is only an assumption and possibly a wrong one.

In short, from whatever angle we consider the matter, we always return to the same basic point. It is that the possibilities of improving the national income or the balance of payments by fostering the national merchant marine, or, more generally, Cuba's maritime activities, are quite limited. Furthermore, by trying to force the pace, one would actually run the risk of obtaining negative results.

A Realistic Maritime Development Policy for Cuba

"A hard look at the facts, or a look at the hard facts" is necessary, according to W. Gorter,[16] for an analysis of maritime policies. That was the aim of this study. But to study questions of fact and to present the results objectively is, for the economist, not the same as to decide what policy should be followed. Below, therefore, we shall try to outline a possible course of action which might result in the orderly development of Cuba's merchant marine.

We have tried to describe the facts of Cuba's maritime transport economy in such a way as to highlight, as clearly as we knew how, the basic characteristics of the domestic maritime activity. In essence they are the following: Cuban shipping concerns have obtained a substantial share of the available traffic in spite of their small size, largely because they operate with chartered vessels. This feature is most important; it has allowed them to make maximum use of their rather limited resources and to exploit fully their greatest, albeit intangible, asset, namely their entrepreneurial, organizational, executive, and administrative capacity. Thus they have also managed to overcome the serious cost problem created by the present structure of the Cuban labor market.

Any public policy must usually be some sort of a compromise, especially when it includes more political than economic elements, as is the case in such matters as we are considering. The economist may have doubts, small ones or great ones,

16. *United States Shipping Policy*, p. 10.

about the usefulness and adequacy of a policy and it will be his duty to state and justify them fully, so that others can appraise and evaluate his position. But once he has performed this duty, he will do well to understand that scientific arguments will not—and perhaps should not—be the only ones that settle the matter. Nor will the vested interests that pressure for a particular policy—in this case the development of the national merchant marine—suddenly cease and desist.

This being so, it may be necessary for the economist to indicate the main features of a policy that at least will not fly openly in the face of the structural realities of the economy at large and of the particular sector that is to be directly affected. A policy meant to foster Cuba's merchant marine must be designed to adhere as closely as possible to the feature that has largely determined the success of the existing industry, that is to say, the practice of using chartered vessels more extensively than self-owned ships. We have already explained that this practice arises from the need to convert fixed costs into variable ones wherever possible. Thus firms can not only expand their volume of operations, but also reduce it in accord with the serious fluctuations to which the demand for the service is subject. With sugar as the only important export freight, operators who want to share in Cuba's traffic have—except on some secondary routes—no choice but to carry this commodity, unless they attempted to do the impossible and tried to devote themselves exclusively to the transportation of the more stable, regular, and remunerative import items. If they should do this, rates would rise to such abnormally high levels that the entry of other competitors could not be prevented.

Thus, the necessity of transporting sugar as the main export cargo determines the need for tramp operators in a business in which small market variations produce large price (rate) fluctuations. And to operate this tramp service with their own ships is impossible for these firms because of their limited

size. There is no other reason why these firms have recourse
to charter-hire for their supply of vessels, and why the traffic
is largely carried under foreign flags. This is the heart of the
matter; all other aspects, except perhaps the cost of crews
protected by Cuban labor and social legislation, are secondary. Even the wage differential, in spite of its undoubted
importance in particular cases, might be overcome by means
of understandings among the interested parties if it were truly
the main obstacle.

Generally speaking therefore, credit facilities for acquiring
ships are not an effective device to aid the industry, although
they may be helpful in the case of some highly specialized
vessels or of boats needed for the transport of goods required
by particular users. The purchased ship would usually have
to be new, its price would be high and so therefore would its
amortization and interest charges. And although the price fluctuations of such vessels in the world market, while not negligible, are not too violent, the freight rates of the principal
cargoes that make up Cuba's exports are extremely volatile.
Nor can one ignore the variations that can always occur in
the volume and composition of Cuba's imports. It follows that
while only in exceptional circumstances might very great losses
be incurred in the capital value of newly bought vessels, and
while over the lifetime of a ship such losses would usually
be offset by gains, it is still entirely possible that during a
substantial slump in freight rates small scale operators might
face insolvency. In such a situation their current revenues
might be insufficient to meet the deferred obligations incurred
when the vessels were bought on credit. The more experienced the operator and the higher his commercial standards,
the more carefully will he consider whether to seek such
credits. In general, we venture to assert, the risks are excessive
except in cases of relatively cheap vessels and of operators
with strong financial positions.

Except in very particular and somewhat varying circum-

stances, credit facilities are thus not the best means for increasing the share of ships sailing under Cuban flag in the
fleets of national operators. The solution must rather be to
maintain the existing specialization. The dichotomy between
the owner and the operator, as it exists today, is a logical
and natural consequence of Cuba's international freight market
and should be tampered with as little as possible.

A solution could consist in having Cuban ownership of the
vessels vested in an institution that is well enough endowed
to face the fluctuations of the time-charter market. Such an
institution would not have to fear the passing risks of periods
of low activity and could maintain itself until the next boom
afforded it the opportunity to recoup its losses. It could hire
out its own ships to operators, and thus a policy to develop
a national fleet could be pursued without direct intervention
in the economy. This policy would fit the existing structure of
the industry and would not interfere with the success of existing firms; rather, it would make use of these firms' best assets,
their experience, their organization, and their links with the
very complex maritime business. These assets have been gathered at great cost, through many trials and errors, and with
much dedication. They should not be wasted.

The ship-owning organization would offer its vessels on the
charter market, both to national and to foreign operators. The
former would thus be denied the special privilege of an oligopsonistic position. Alternatively, charters might only be
granted to Cuban operators, but at the rates prevailing in the
world market. It might even be possible to devise formulae
for charters that would offer incentives for the operators to
acquire the vessels. The ship-owning organization would make
profits or losses according to the state of the charter market,
but if its vessels possess the characteristics needed for their
adequate utilization and are rented out to solvent and experienced operators, the losses should, in the long run, be offset
by profits. An experiment with this method of protecting and

aiding the national merchant fleet would, we think, be preferable to those usually proposed.[17]

The ship-owning organization would not be burdened with the complicated and costly business of soliciting freights, moving vessels, etc. If wage bargains were negotiated with the crew or their representatives, it may be hoped that tolerable levels of pay could be achieved and that these would have some flexibility, even if not as much as charter-hire freight rates. There is no doubt that even under these circumstances a policy to foster the national merchant marine would encounter serious difficulties. But as long as one proceeds in a responsible and deliberate manner, there is no doubt that in the course of time these will sort themselves out and solutions can be found that will not prejudice the interests of any party with a bona fide concern in the matter. It will never be economically possible for Cuba to launch a great merchant fleet, but a cautious trial-and-error approach will permit us to test how much may in fact be feasible.

17. See for instance Eloy Gonzalez's study, "El Transporte Marítimo Nacional: Base para su Desarrollo y Consolidación" ("The National Maritime Transport: Basis for its Development and Consolidation") in the volume *Conferencia para el Progreso de la Economía Nacional.* The author shows an adequate knowledge of the national shipping business but, unfortunately, bases his case on a superficial and quite mistaken interpretation of the significance of freights in Cuba's balance of international payments on ocean transport account. The same error is made in *La Conferencia de Seattle y la Solución Cubana* (*The Seattle Conference and the Cuban Solution*), Havana 1946, prepared by the operators' delegation (J. L. Coterillo, Engineer).

CONCLUSIONS

FROM THE PRECEDING PRESENTATION the following conclusions emerge. They are presented in summary form only for the purpose of recapitulation and not necessarily in their order of importance.

1. *Cuba's international ocean freight traffic is large in volume and in value, but is exceedingly concentrated on trade routes to the United States. Export and import cargoes are not in balance.*

Since Cuba has an open economy, i.e., one with a large foreign sector, its international commodity trade yields large payloads. This, and the island character of the country, both justify and require the already existing excellent and ample maritime transport services. But it is important to note that the tonnage shipped abroad vastly exceeds that imported, and that this imbalance increases when liquid cargoes are excluded from the calculation. And the high concentration of trade between Cuba and the United States makes for an even greater imbalance in the traffic between Cuba and the rest of the world.

2. *The characteristics of export freight differ from those of imports. This in turn makes for differences in the respective transport markets and freight structures.*

Discounting liquid cargoes, which are mainly molasses on the export side and fuels (petroleum or gasoline) on the import side, Cuba's dry cargo exports are mainly sugar (raw and refined) and, secondarily, minerals. The remainder consists of

179

a variety of products, most of them agricultural. These commodities are usually sent in bulk shipments by tramp or free navigation freighters. The market for the services of such vessels is decidedly competitive.

Dry cargo imports, on the other hand, are largely manufactured goods, transported by regular liners travelling along routes serviced by a small number of firms. These firms tend to enter into oligopolistic "conference" agreements to establish uniform freight rates. The imperfection of this market is a response to inescapable economic pressures which make it necessary to order and regulate the competition among such shipping concerns.

Freight rates for export commodities are subject to violent and sudden fluctuations which are caused by changes in the demand for the products themselves and by the low elasticity of the supply of ships. Import freights, established by conferences, on the other hand, are remarkably stable over time.

3. *The production costs of ocean transport service are distinguished by the heavy weight of fixed costs. This fact is important in a variety of ways.*

Shipping concerns are notable examples of firms operating under increasing returns precisely because of the high proportion of fixed costs to total costs. Substantial economies of scale can therefore be gained as the enterprise grows in size. This, in turn, makes modestly endowed firms, such as Cuba's, turn to the use of chartered vessels rather than operate their own ships. In this lies one of the most characteristic features of the Cuban firms already in the business.

4. *Costs and freight rates are closely related in Cuba's international ocean traffic. The monopolistic market structure of the transport of imports does not result in rates greatly in excess of the cost of producing the service.*

Since the market is competitive, export freight rates closely follow the cost of producing the service. Import freight rates are determined in monopolistic markets in which both supply and demand are strongly influenced by the bargaining power of operators and shippers. The latter often are oligopsonists.

5. *A rigorous economic analysis of the components of Cuba's balance of international payments on ocean freight transport account shows that the present structure of this balance is not susceptible to major changes, and that any attempt to induce them would not be advisable from an economic point of view.*

If from gross freights we subtract freight handling charges (loading, unloading, pier, etc.) and those other items whose influence on the balance of payments is not affected by the nationality of the owners of the vessels, we obtain what might be called freight payments proper. These are very much smaller than is usually thought. In the final analysis, only the net pay of crews and the net profits—if any—of the operators would give Cuba a more favorable balance of payments if national operators gained an even greater share of the total traffic than they already had in 1958.

6. *The effects on the national income of a policy by which a Cuban merchant fleet would be fostered would also be so negligible as not to justify such a policy.*

Since Cuba already has an abundance of maritime services, the only contributions which a Cuban merchant fleet could make to the national income would be those mentioned in relation to the balance of payments, namely the wages of labor and the profits of the firms. But the capital investments needed for a given increase in the national fleet would yield smaller additions to employment and to labor income than would similar investments in other lines of production. In turn, the always precarious profits of operators would become even more doubtful because of the high costs implied in operating under the Cuban flag. And widening Cuba's maritime activities by installing shipyards in which the additional vessels would be built would probably worsen the situation and make a maritime development policy more difficult and complex.

7. *If, because of non-economic considerations, a program to expand the merchant fleet under the Cuban flag is unavoidable, it should at least be well designed so as to make maximum use of what already exists. Possibly the best plan would be to endow some public institution with funds to enable it to become the owner of ships sailing under the national flag. These it would rent out to operators—especially, but not exclusively, Cuban operators—under time charters.*

This proposal distinguishes between the owner and the operator, and thereby would allow the maintenance of the present structure of the industry in Cuba. The existing specialization with respect to functions and risks would thus remain unaltered. The owning entity, quasi-public in character, would concentrate its activities on making ships available. In this respect it would be responsible for resolving the special problems, particularly in labor relations, which sailing under the Cuban flag involves, so that these problems would not constitute a major constraint on the operators. But it would be free from all responsibility in the complicated business of obtaining, handling, and transporting freight.

This would be a policy of coordination which would avoid a ruinous competition between the existing private companies and the public sector's efforts to create a national merchant fleet. Such damaging competition, unfortunately, is already making itself felt.

Index

INDEX

Administration. *See* Management and administration

Advertising. *See* Sales promotion

Air transport, 14, 79n, 107

"Bahia" ships, 128, 129n

Balance of payment, Cuba's: effect of ferries on, 107–8n; method of calculating, 108–10; revenues and expenditures, 111–13, 117–19, 119–22; data for 1957–58, 133–42; effect of merchant marine on, 147, 167, 174; and shipyards, 169, 173; susceptibility to change, 181; mentioned, 3, 55, 161

Belgium, 10

Britain. *See* Great Britain

British Royal Commission on Shipping, 34

Canada, 10

Cargo: special handling of, 6, 57–58, 97, 99, 101, 126, 127; of tramp vessels, 29; carried at a loss, 102–3; and ship construction, 153. *See also* Exports, Cuban; Imports, Cuban; names of individual products

— dry: tonnage of, 5–6, 78, 113–14; geographic distribution of, 6–7, 8–13; shipped to U.S., 7; exported, 36–44; imported, 44–50; and freight rates, 47, 97; entering Havana, 53, 78; composition of, 179

— liquid: tonnage of, 5–6, 113–14; specialized transport of, 7–8; exported, 36–44; mentioned, 179

Cattle, transport of, 157

Cereals, transport of, 17, 29, 38, 152, 153

Ceylon, 165

Charter service: and market, 17–18, 45; and freight rates, 30–31, 40, 101–2, 128, 138; advantages and disadvantages of, 57, 84–91, 175; and contract length, 138–39, 140–41; vessels for, 138, 177; and Cuba's maritime policy, 174–75, 182; mentioned, 82, 93, 108

Cimavi vessels, 140

Coal, transport of, 6, 17, 29, 38, 45, 136, 137

Coffee, transport of, 9

Commissions, 121–22, 126

Competition: effect on rates, 16, 20, 35, 43–44, 51–52; and conferences, 19–20, 23–25, 46, 93; and specialization, 28–30, 95; in tramp market, 30–31; in liner market, 32–33, 34; in fruit and vegetable market, 42–44; kinds of, 49–50, 51; tools of, 52; and sales promotion, 64–65; among commodities, 93; and management, 93–94; and costs, 103; regulation of, 180; mentioned, 40, 182

Conferences: described, 19–20; as oligopolistic agreements, 20, 21–27, 180; and freight rates, 28, 34–35, 47–48, 128, 141, 180; and Cuban imports, 45; and competition, 46, 93; list of, 47

Consignment fees, 119

Costs of maritime freight transport: and vessel capacity, 53; and distance and route, 56, 61–62; fixed and variable, 56–60, 62–63, 175, 180–81; and vessels, 59, 60, 62, 63, 84–91, 101–3, 128–30, 132, 133; transit expenditures, 59, 60, 62, 63, 108, 130, 131–32; and management, 61;